LONE STAR

REEL WEST

REEL WEST

ANDREW PATRICK NELSON, SERIES EDITOR

Reel West is a unique series of short, neatly packaged volumes exploring individual western films across the whole history of the canon, from early and classic westerns to revisionist and spaghetti westerns. The series considers the many themes and variations that have accrued over more than a century of this most American of film styles. Intended for general readers as well as for classroom use, these brief books will offer smart, incisive examinations of the aesthetic, cultural, experiential, and personal meaning and legacy of the films they discuss and will provide strong arguments for their importance—all filtered through the consciousness of writers of distinction from within the disciplines of film criticism, journalism, and literature.

Also available in the Reel West:

The Man Who Shot Libery Vaalance by Chris Yogerst
Broken Arrow by Angela Aleiss
Ride the High Country by Robert Nott
Thelma & Louise by Susan Kollin
Ride Lonesome by Kirk Ellis
Blood on the Moon by Alan K. Rode

LONE STAR

ALISON FIELDS

University of New Mexico Press ∩ Albuquerque

Printed in the United States of America

ISBN 978-0-8263-6939-0 (paper)
ISBN 978-0-8263-6940-6 (ePub)

Library of Congress Control Number: 2025946086

Founded in 1889, the University of New Mexico sits on the traditional homelands of the Pueblo of Sandia. The original peoples of New Mexico—Pueblo, Navajo, and Apache—since time immemorial have deep connections to the land and have made significant contributions to the broader community statewide. We honor the land itself and those who remain stewards of this land throughout the generations and also acknowledge our committed relationship to Indigenous peoples. We gratefully recognize our history.

Cover illustration: still from *Lone Star*
Series design by Felicia Cedillos
Composited by Isaac Morris
Composed in Adobe Jenson 9.5/13.75

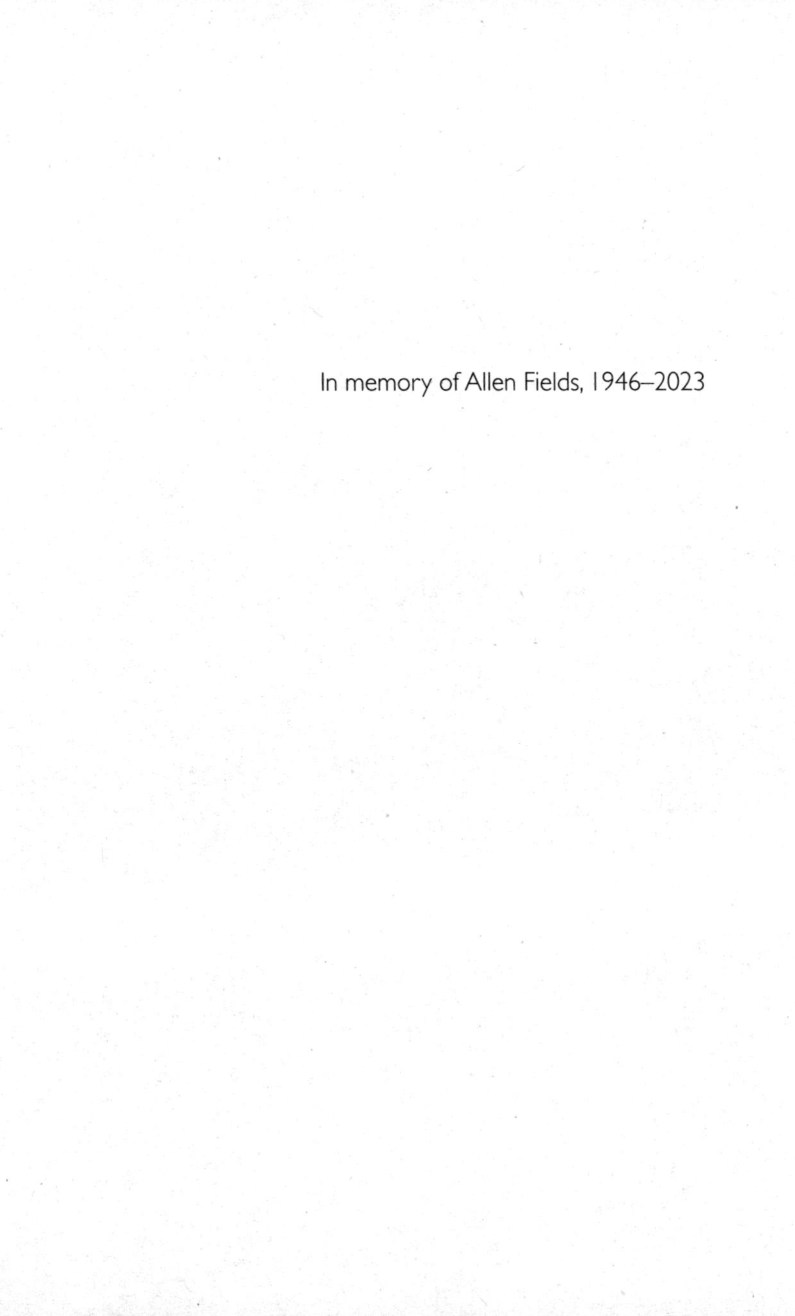

In memory of Allen Fields, 1946–2023

CONTENTS

ILLUSTRATIONS

ACKNOWLEDGMENTS

When Andrew Patrick Nelson invited me to consider contributing a manuscript to his Reel West series at the University of New Mexico Press, I immediately thought of John Sayles's *Lone Star*. Beginning my first year as an art history professor at the University of Oklahoma fifteen years ago, I developed as one of my first courses one entitled Cinema of the American West; ever since, *Lone Star* has remained a staple of the course syllabus. I have always been intrigued by the film's treatment of legend, history, memory, and transnationalism in the American West. The opportunity of digging more fully into *Lone Star* by exploring its key themes, production history, critical reception, and ongoing legacy has been a welcome pleasure.

I am thankful to Andrew Patrick Nelson and Stephen Hull at the University of New Mexico Press for including my work in this series, as well as to the project's peer reviewers. In this endeavor, I relied on the assistance of Philip Hallman, Film Studies Field Librarian and Curator of the Screen Arts Mavericks & Makers Collection, and Linda Skolarus, Research Services Librarian at the Special Collections Research Center at the University of Michigan, who helped to maximize my time with the institution's John Sayles papers. Two University of Oklahoma graduate research assistants provided valuable support at differing stages of this project. Tom Kahle provided initial research support, while Abby Mikalauskas assisted throughout the production process. I also thank my students for so many enriching conversations over the years and my colleagues and administrators in the School of Visual Arts for supporting my research activity. As ever, I am so appreciative of my mother, Linda Fields, who encouraged me through this project and provided copyediting assistance, and of my son, Asher. This book is dedicated to the memory of my father, Allen Fields, who grew up on Western films and was always my biggest supporter.

LONE STAR

Introduction

Lone Star had its origins in John Sayles's first visit to the Alamo. While in San Marcos, Texas, where he was working on the 1978 horror film *Piranha,* he used a day off to visit the iconic San Antonio landmark. There, a band of Texans, along with James Bowie, Davy Crockett, and William B. Travis, held off General Antonio López de Santa Anna's Centralist army for thirteen days, before falling on the morning of March 6, 1836. Since those days, the Alamo has become a symbol of American sacrifice in the name of freedom. Commander-in-chief of the Texas army, Sam Houston invoked the loss, shouting "Remember the Alamo!" when his forces decisively defeated Santa Anna at the battle of San Jacinto, a little over a month later.

The Alamo story has been repeatedly reproduced in literature and film, transforming the battle from "a site of defeat in 1836 to a powerfully rendered and racially produced icon of American cultural memory,"[1] that solidified beliefs about Anglo and Mexican racial difference.[2] As a foundational legend in Texas, the Alamo in its popular representations celebrates freedom-seeking Anglos in contrast to their criminally vicious Mexican rivals.[3] Chicana writer and activist Gloria Anzaldúa argues that the battle became a symbol that "legitimized the white imperialist takeover," beginning with the formation of the Republic of Texas.[4] Before being annexed by the United States in 1846, the independent republic was represented by a flag with a single star on it, leading to Texas's lasting nickname of the Lone Star State.

Sayles himself had grown up watching the 1954 Disney television miniseries *Davy Crockett*, starring Fess Parker, and the heroic 1960 battle film *The Alamo*, directed by and starring John Wayne as Davy Crockett, but on the day of his visit Chicano protestors were circling the mission, questioning "Why don't you tell the whole story?"[5] The protestors explained to Sayles that the fight for Texas freedom also was an attempt to retain the institution of slavery, which had been outlawed in Mexico. Sayles recognized that the question of slavery had been omitted from Texas history books, along with other complexities of the story of the Alamo. The encounter prompted him to contemplate how certain histories have been silenced in the production of official narratives.[6]

In John Ford's 1962 *The Man Who Shot Liberty Valance*, having just discovered that Random Stoddard (James Stewart) had not actually killed Liberty Valance, a reporter for the Shinbone Star famously concludes, "When legend becomes fact, print the legend." *Valance* suggests that at both a local and national level, identity and progress involve suppressing certain narratives in favor of unifying legends.[7] Similarly, *Lone Star* features a town whose identity hinges on a mythic fabrication—the legend of Sheriff Buddy Deeds. Both films offer a mediation of the relationship between history and memory, and how legends are solidified in official narratives. For Sayles, one key question is this: "What happens when your legends are not useful anymore, they're actually holding you back?"[8] *Lone Star* deliberates whether it is possible to leave history behind, to "Forget the Alamo."[9] Ultimately Sayles suggests that to move forward "you've really got to examine your legends and revise them toward the true complexity of the situation."[10] This complexity reveals that, unlike the title image of the Lone Star or the polarizing legend of the Alamo, personal and communal histories are tied together often more closely than we may want to acknowledge.[11]

PLOT AND GENRE

Directed, written, and edited by John Sayles, an American independent filmmaker, the Western film *Lone Star* was released in 1996. Set in the present-day fictional small town of Frontera on the Texas/Mexico border, the film opens with the discovery of a decades-old skeleton on a rifle range, the remains of the racist and corrupt former sheriff, Charley Wade (Kris Kristofferson). It had long been presumed that Wade was driven from town by Buddy Deeds (Matthew McConaughey), a former deputy who succeeded him for a long tenure as Frontera's beloved sheriff. The discovery of Wade's remains prompts current sheriff Sam Deeds (Chris Cooper), who had always lived in his father's shadow, to question Buddy's legacy and his involvement in Wade's death. Sam's investigation into his father's past leads to the resurfacing of other long buried secrets. He reconnects with Pilar Cruz (Elizabeth Pena), his forbidden teenage love, whom he ultimately discovers is his half-sister—born of an affair between Buddy and Pilar's mother, Mercedes Cruz (Miriam Colon). Sam learns that Mercedes's husband Eladio was murdered by Wade for smuggling migrants across the border, and that after Wade's disappearance, Buddy embezzled county funds to help Mercedes open a restaurant in Frontera. Now a respected business owner and councilwoman, Mercedes casts the deciding vote in naming the town's courthouse after Buddy. The contested courthouse dedication highlights competing voices in Frontera and further spurs Sam's investigation. Sam questions Mayor Hollis Pogue (Clifton James), another former deputy who repeatedly warns him to leave the past alone, and Otis Payne (Ron Canada), the owner of Big-O's, a bar serving the town's African American community. Otis's estranged son, lieutenant colonel Delmore Payne (Joe Morton), has recently returned to Frontera to lead its soon-to-close army base, offering Otis the opportunity to meet his grandson, Chet (Eddie Robinson). While anchored by a murder mystery, *Lone Star* investigates a series of interconnected family histories, as well as Frontera's simmering racial and political tensions. Sayles positions Frontera on the cusp of social and institutional change, prompted by a series of border crossings and multicultural encounters.

With more than fifty speaking parts, and an intricate, bilingual, and time-shifting narrative, *Lone Star* challenges easy genre categorization. Critics have often labeled the film a neo-Western that brings Western themes into a contemporary setting. It is set in southwest Texas, characters wear cowboy hats and boots, and the film focuses a lot on law and order. However, Kimberly Sulze notes that "from the outset, it is clear that we are not in cinematically familiar terrain—either in the Hollywood sense or in the classical Western genre sense. The visual portrayal of the landscape is different, the use of sound is different, and so are the characterizations."[12] That is, *Lone Star* eschews grand landscape shots, much of the sound comes from the world of the film, and characters are notably diverse.

Lone Star's depiction of the West as multicultural has led some to describe the film as a revisionist western. However, Sayles does not view the film this way. He has said, "As far as I'm concerned, it is not revisionism to included Mexican American culture or African-American

Figure 1. John Sayles provides direction to Chris Cooper.

culture or any of the many other different groups. If you're talking about the history of the United States, you're always talking about those things, from the get-go."[13] However, films in the Western genre were not intended as reflection of the past itself, "but rather our contemporary idealized version of the past," meant to reflect current values.[14] Lee Clark Mitchell cautions that "no stable version of a genre transcends a particular moment, since genres are always being reshaped by each new potential member," and that the Western genre has constantly changed over time.[15] However, Sayles intentionally breaks from the "formula stories that have a proven audience and track record."[16]

Lone Star's departure from the Western formula occurs in several ways. In Western films, wearing a badge "typically mean[s] . . . represent[ing] goodness and responsibility," a signal that justice will be enforced.[17] However, the first badge shown in *Lone Star*, half buried in the dirt, is the one that belonged to Charley Wade, a character antithetical to heroism. Further, Western films often focus on solitary protagonists, usually white males, who are called upon to restore order to a community, but never truly become part of it—among them, those in films such as George Steven's *Shane* (1953), Ford's *The Searchers* (1956), and Clint Eastwood's *The Outlaw Josey Wales* (1976). In contrast, *Lone Star* follows multiple characters, representing Anglos, Mexican Americans, and African Americans in central storylines. Tarancón Juan Francisco writes that unlike the classic Western, the structure of *Lone Star* recognizes "the many diverse experiences of the different people that inhabit the West create a kaleidoscopic vision of the past where not one, but many paths crisscross to create a complex, vibrant and multifaceted vision of present U.S. society."[18] Rather than reinforcing fixed Western narratives of Anglo frontier triumph, manifest destiny, and rugged individualism, the focus of *Lone Star* is on "contact, exchange and hybridization."[19]

In the American Studies Association presidential addresses delivered in 1997, Mary Helen Washington takes up *Lone Star*'s representation of a multicultural society as what one character refers to as a "damn menudo." Sayles, Washington argues, creates a "cinematic menudo" through his representation of border crossings and "inter-racial and inter-ethnic exchanges." She writes, "Sayles's menudo represents the multicultural moment as a messy, contentious process in which the resolution of disputes is not as important as the freer play of long-silenced voices."[20] This approach places "the cultural myth of white supremacy" under critique; it also places in view "Sayles's vision of south Texas as the multi-racial, multi-ethnic world he says it has always been. Black, Hispanic, and Native American cultural threads are woven—and interwoven—so pervasively into the texture of the film that visually, aurally, and linguistically these cross-stitchings become the cultural norm that frames the action of Sayles's characters."[21] The following year, Janice Radway built on Washington's address by suggesting that *Lone Star* models a vision for the field of American Studies that resists the "premature closure" that can occur in a search for a "distinctively American 'common ground.'"[22]

Sayles's "cinematic menudo" stylistically draws from multiple genres, echoing texts ranging "from classic westerns, border movies, film noir, murder mysteries, to Mexican American writing."[23] In addition to the parallels with Ford's *Valance*, Neil Campbell notes that *Lone Star* also pays homage to Orson Welles's *Touch of Evil* (1968), a film that represents the border "as a space of complex exchange and porosity, where corruption and the law are entwined like the very histories of the people who live there."[24] In *Touch*, a well-known example of film noir, information is revealed to the viewer from multiple perspectives, including, slowly, the extent of Hank Quinlan's corruption. Robert M. Young's *The Ballad of Gregorio Cortez* (1982) tells and retells the story of the same event—the shooting of a Karnes County sheriff by Mexican American farmer after a misunderstanding—through its use of the multiple perspectives of its storytellers. In unravelling *Lone Star*'s central murder mystery, key information likewise comes in pieces, the effect of which fragments a linear storyline. Perhaps the most notable cinematic device Sayles employs in *Lone Star* is his use of live segues (discussed in detail in chapter 2), which are continuous pan shots that are used to create continuity between past and present. There are no dissolves, fades, or other usual cinematic markers—a technique loosely inspired by Welles.[25] Sayles's approach requires patience from the audience, as watching it is like entering the world of a long novel.

Lone Star's runtime is two hours fifteen minutes, and is largely absent of violence, sex, or action scenes. Amid the heavy dialogue, multiple voices overlap at times and thus demand careful listening.[26] Sayles has described his desire to challenge audiences who are accustomed to mainstream films that provide tidy explanations and, "to an extent, where your genre expectations are always met." While he consciously uses some characters as relatable to provide a connection point for the audience, his deeper concern is to "tell the story completely and not in shorthand," giving each character their full due.[27] Melissa Clark Jones observes that Sayles "avoids stereotypic or cardboard characters, manipulative plot twists, special effects, and overly polemical or dramatic solutions. Instead, his characters come to their personal transformations and understandings through narratively overlapping micro-epics." Through this approach, he "creatively revises the audience's experience of traditional genres, history, and heroism."[28] Despite his diversion from set formulas, Sayles harnesses the power of genre conventions and the persistence of the West's frontier myth, recognizing that both provide important points of entry and connection for audiences. Sultze suggests that Sayles was able to work in such a manner because of his marginalization in the Hollywood system.[29]

JOHN SAYLES, FILMMAKER

As an acclaimed independent director, writer, and novelist, Sayles has been recognized as one of the most important contemporary filmmakers depicting American culture. With a career that now spans almost fifty years, he began working as a novelist and, early in his film career, as a screenwriter of monster movies for director Roger Corman on films such as *Piranha, Alligator* (1980) and *The Howling* (1981). His debut as a director was on the microbudget 1980 *Return Of The Secaucus 7*. This film follows a group of college friends reuniting at a New Hampshire summer house, which some commentators have likened to *The Big Chill*. He further built his reputation with ensuing films, *Brother from Another Planet* (1984), *Matewan* (1987; also starring Chris Cooper), *Eight Men Out* (1988), *City of Hope* (1991), *Passion Fish* (1992), and *The Secret of Roan Inish* (1995). Shortly after *Lone Star*, Sayles went on to direct *Men with Guns* (1997), a Latin American political drama filmed in Mexico in Spanish and Mayan.

From *Matewan*, portraying a 1920s coal mining strike in West Virginia, to *Passion Fish*, which follows an injured actress's return to her home in the Louisiana bayou, Sayles trains his attention on regional specificity, focusing on the competing interests and voices of the communities he depicts. Some of his more recent novels, such as *Yellow Earth* (2020), set during an oil boom in North Dakota, and *Jamie MacGillivray: A Renegade's Journey* (2023), which moves from the Scottish highlands to colonial America, are expansive in scope, yet remain deeply tied to local histories.

Sayles often directs, writes, and edits his films, finalizing production from his garage at his farm in upstate New York, where he lives with his producing and life partner, Maggie Renzi. When Sayles accepted funding for his 1983 film, *Baby It's You*, and then was not able to make the changes on the final cut, he committed to retaining creative control on his projects.[30] To be able to self-finance projects, he took work as a Hollywood script doctor, reshaping scripts for films such as 1995's *The Quick and the Dead* and *Apollo 13*. When questioned about why he has avoided making films in the Hollywood system, Sayles responded, "It seems to be a mutual decision," noting a misalignment between the stories he wanted to tell and the films that Hollywood sold.[31] *Lone Star* earned Sayles his second Academy Award nomination for best screenplay (following *Passion Fish*) and remains the most critically celebrated of his films.

The script for *Lone Star* was bound up with Sayles's exposure to and expectations regarding Texas history, from early television and film about the Alamo, to a hitchhiking trip he took across the country in his early twenties. When he traveled through Texas, he was surprised to find that the borderline between the United States and Mexico did not neatly divide Anglo English speakers and Mexican Spanish speakers in the ways he had pictured. Over time, Sayles became "fascinated with the idea of the history of Texas as a very compressed metaphor for U.S. history," with the state's revolution, civil war, and reconstruction occurring within twenty-five years.[32] He began to imagine a story that would include different cultural groups along the border, as well as the state's violent history—in his resolute belief that in Texas, the story "had to be about murder."[33]

In writing the screenplay as a murder mystery, Sayles was inspired by the work of the American-British novelist Raymond Chandler, who used detective stories to illuminate aspects of race and politics in America. He said, "So for me, that [premise] that there's been a murder and 'who did it,' sent me off on an interesting story about our border, Texas specifically, but also about borders in general."[34] Once committed to the story, Sayles wrote quickly, completing a draft in a couple of months. He did not initially have the resolution of who shot Wade, but as in Chandler's novels, the resolution of the murder mystery was not the point.[35]

Once Sayles wrote *Lone Star*, he attained financing from Castle Rock Entertainment, a film and television production company founded in 1987 as a subsidiary of Warner Bros. Pictures, the five-million-dollar budget significantly larger than any of his prior films. While it was a departure to accept outside funding, Sayles had confidence in working with Castle Rock due to his prior work writing a film for director Rob Reiner, a cofounder of the company. He explained, "They are a company formed by filmmakers and not businessmen, agents and deal makers. They understand that you make the commitment to the screenplay and the filmmaker."[36] A production company, Rio Dulce, was formed as the legal entity for *Lone Star*. Maggie Renzi and Paul Miller served as coproducers, John Sloss served executive producer, and a streamlined crew of about fifty was employed on the film.

CAST

In a book about the production of *Matewan*, Sayles claims, "Cast a movie well and half your troubles are over." If characters are engaging and believably presented, he writes, the audience will overlook many other shortcomings in a film.[37] The comparatively larger budget for *Lone Star* allowed Sayles more freedom in his casting selections. At its center are three generations of white Texas sheriffs—Charley Wade, Buddy Deeds, and Sam Deeds—each representing a very different approach to law and order. In casting these characters, Sayles, casting director Avy

Kaufman, and the production team selected three actors with ties to Texas.

Identifying Kris Kristofferson to play the villainous Wade required him to play against type, but Sayles recognized that "Kris Kristofferson is not only from Texas; he's from the border. He knows that world. He knows that music. He knows those redneck sheriffs."[38] Born in Brownsville, Texas, Kristofferson's father was a major general in the US Air Force. After his family moved to California, Kristofferson graduated with a degree in literature and won a Rhodes scholarship to study at Oxford. He joined the US Army and advanced in rank before leaving for a songwriting career in Nashville.[39] A singer and songwriter who wrote for hundreds of artists, including Johnny Cash ("Sunday Morning Coming Down") and Janis Joplin ("Me and Bobby McGee"), Kristofferson became part of the country supergroup The Highwaymen and was inducted into the Country Music Hall of Fame in 2004. Beginning in the 1970s, he found a concurrent second career in film and acted in more than fifty films. He starred in Sam Peckinpah's *Pat Garrett & Billy the Kid* (1973), in Martin Scorsese's *Alice Doesn't Live Here Anymore* (1974), and in Frank Pierson's *A Star is Born* (1976).[40] After the outsize box office failure of Michael Cimino's epic western *Heaven's Gate* (1980), Kristofferson's film career slowed somewhat, but *Lone Star* presented a new kind of role. Although he had never been cast as a bad guy before, Kristofferson's gravelly voice and imposing screen presence made him an effective villain.

In casting Matthew McConaughey as Buddy Deeds, Sayles was looking for someone with the screen presence to play off Kristofferson but without the weight of celebrity status. At the time, McConaughey had appeared in only one film—Richard Linklater's *Dazed and*

Confused. One of Sayles's favorite parts of that film was "that laid-back Texan, that 'just keep living' guy."[41] Sayles learned that McConaughey was a film student from Ulvade, Texas, with an easy familiarity with the borderlands. McConaughey's turn as Buddy was quickly followed by a starring role in Joel Schumacher's adaptation of John Grisham's *A Time to Kill*, which was also released in 1996. That role placed McConaughey amid a major publicity push, leading Sayles to comment at the time, "Matthew is a good, hard-working young actor and I hope he can survive all the hype."[42] McConaughey appeared to take his growing fame in stride, often appearing on magazine covers with his beloved dog. His cast deal memo for *Lone Star*, under "other," notes: "bringing his dog."[43]

In the 2000s, McConaughey went on to star in a string of romantic comedies, which, though successful, made him feel pigeonholed in his career. He returned to Texas with his family, determined to stay at his Austin ranch until a compelling Hollywood role came along. This strategy ultimately led him to parts in dramas such as Jean-Marc Vallée's *Dallas Buyers Club* (2013), which earned him Academy Award and Golden Globe for best actor.[44] In 2015, McConaughey became a visiting instructor in the Department of Radio-Television-Film at the University of Texas at Austin, before joining the faculty as a Professor of Practice in 2019. He developed curriculum for, and coteaches, a film production course in the department.[45] Both Kristofferson and McConaughey were inducted into the Texas Film Hall of Fame in 2006.

Chris Cooper, who had played key roles in *Matewan* and *City of Hope*, was Sayles's choice for Sam Deeds "because he had that iconic American Gary Cooper thing" and because he had the ability to "play a subtext."[46] As Sam quietly and purposely investigates his father's past, he keeps his expressions guarded and his words few. In these scenes, as one reviewer observed, Cooper's "uncanny ability to express interior states makes his closeups particularly eloquent."[47] Cooper is also a native Texan, with both sides of his family going back generations in the state. He also had experience in the Western genre, having played Sheriff July Johnson in the miniseries *Lonesome Dove* (1989). Cooper would go to win an Academy Award for best supporting actor for his role in Spike Jones's *Adaptation* in 2002.

As the casting of Cooper suggests, Sayles often returned to the same actors for his projects. Cooper later collaborated with Sayles on *Silver City* (2004) and *Amigo* (2010). Echoing the film's three generations of sheriffs, three generations of the Payne family—Otis (Ron Canada), Delmore (Joe Morton) and Chet (Eddie Robinson)—further underscored the theme of strained father/son relationships. Sayles had previously worked with Morton on *The Brother from Another Planet* and *City of Hope*. Miriam Colon, a Puerto Rican actress with a long Broadway, television, and film career, known for playing Al Pacino's mother in *Scarface* (1983) and her role in *City of Hope*, was cast as Mercedes. Elizabeth Peña, a daughter of Cuban immigrants who had been acting since age eight, and who also had starred in a short-lived legal drama created by Sayles, *Shannon's Deal* (1990–1991), was cast as Pilar.

Beyond the core characters, *Lone Star*'s large supporting cast includes "a conservative bartender, illegal immigrants, high school students, a roadside souvenir stand owner, army privates and sergeants, a story-hungry journalist, and a Texas football fanatic."[48] Frances McDormand, who plays a small but memorable role as Bunny Kincaid, Sam's ex-wife, was nominated for a Best Actress Academy Award for her role in *Fargo* in 1996, the same year *Lone Star* was released. Even minor characters experience full narrative arcs, including Enrique (Richard Coca), who plays a busboy at Mercedes's diner. Sayles drew on his own experience as an actor in thinking through these side characters, recalling that no matter the size of the dialogue, a tethering point must exist to the broader story.[49]

MAKING THE FILM

Much of *Lone Star* was shot in Eagle Pass, Texas, a town with a population of under 27,000 in 1995, just across the border from Piedras Negras, Coahuila, in Mexico. Eagle Pass is a small town with fast food restaurants, chain hotels, a mall, and movie theater; the cast and crew set up camp at the local La Quinta Inn. Sayles recognized the importance of accurately portraying this border town. To help avoid any false notes, he drafted extras from the community and selectively shared his script with locals to be sure that place-based details were correct.[50] While the history of Eagle Pass itself was informative, Sayles imagined Frontera as "kind of a composite of a bunch of towns down there."[51]

Most of the film's sets were built from abandoned buildings. The drive-in, the most ambitious set piece, was built from scratch.[52] Reportedly, two million dollars of the total production sum was expended in Maverick County, home of Eagle Pass. This provided a modest boost to the local economy as residents were hired as extras, and living expenses of the cast and crew benefited the county. Even though set in the fictional town of Frontera, residents could easily point out the identifiable Eagle Pass locations from shots of Main Street, the Maverick County Courthouse lawn, and City Hall.[53] Gaining access to certain locations in Eagle Pass also provided Sayles a sense of the town's distribution of wealth—filming locations on the Rio Grande, for instance, required the production company to lease land from wealthy Anglo ranchers.[54]

Figure 2. Eagle Pass, Texas.

Sayles enlisted cinematographer Stuart Dryburgh, who was a recent Academy Award nominee for his work on Jane Campion's 1994 film *The Piano*. Dryburgh, who grew up in New Zealand, was drawn to the opportunity to work in the American Southwest with its arid desert landscape that he had only seen in movies. It seemed a "no brainer" to Dryburgh that the film should be shot in CinemaScope's widescreen anamorphic format, using Panavision cameras and lenses.[55] As one reviewer noted, this format allowed for "the juxtaposition of voids and actors conferring intimacy of a sort quite distinct from that possible in the narrower frame."[56]

The southwest Texas landscape further dictated Dryburgh's approach: Its dusty bleached-out desert infused the film's color, which at times contrasted with the bright fluorescent lights of the diner or school. He was particularly conscious of moving between the two time periods represented. From the timeline suggested in the film, *Lone Star* spans about forty years, moving from the late 1950s, with the disappearance of Wade and Buddy's appointment to sheriff in 1957, to present-day mid-1990s, following Buddy's death in 1991.[57]

The film's music also created a bridge between time periods and cultures. At times, the present-day scenes are scored with music from the past, providing subtext, or a "gut feeling" to the audience.[58] *Lone Star*'s musical director was Mason Daring, a frequent Sayles collaborator. Beginning the film, Sayles sat down with Daring to discuss the film's philosophy. Daring both created original compositions for the film and secured rights to a mixture of Spanish, black, and white rock and blues. The resulting musical selections, from artists such as Los Lobos, Lucinda Williams, Freddie Fender, Little Walter, Big Joe Turner, Little Willie John, Chelo Silva, and Patsy Montana, underscore "the mix and flux of culture."[59]

This mix and flux become obvious when Delmore walks into his father's club early in the film, and black singer-songwriter and pianist Ivory Joe Hunter's 1950s rhythm-and-blues hit "Since I Met You Baby" plays in the background. Later, in what Washington identifies as the "Rock-en-Español" scene, Sam and Pilar meet at the Santa Barbara Café after hours and restart their romance. Pilar walks to the jukebox, noting "my mother hasn't changed the songs since I was ten." When she makes her selection, viewers hear the opening bars to Hunter's song, but the musician this time is Freddie Fender singing "Desde Que Conozco," a rock-en-Español cover of the original song. While Washington notes that this is a "minor example of cultural exchange," "it [also] shows an African-American-Chicano cross-cultural sharing, that at least on the level of art-music, represents a first step."[60] Sayles's soundtrack selection highlights this cultural exchange, with music functioning to quietly support the film's thematic points. He explains, "You don't have to know the history to feel it underneath. Music and sports are very often where cultures meet first, where they blend."[61]

While Western films often have prominent scores to cue emotional responses, much of *Lone Star*'s sound is diegetic, coming directly from characters and their surroundings—for instance, music in the nightclub or the jukebox at the Santa Barbara Café.[62] Notable exceptions include a forensics montage set to Tex-Mex music and Sam's drive to the café, set to Little Willie John's "My Love Is." A significant portion of the film's budget was used to secure music rights, yet Sayles and Daring still faced restrictions. The soundtrack, which was originally to include twenty-seven songs, was ultimately whittled down to twenty-two due to budget constraints.[63]

Lone Star was filmed over the course of thirty-nine days. Scenes were shot out of order, beginning with the dedication of the memorial for Buddy and concluding with a reshoot of Sam's last dialogue at Big O's. This order of filming was dictated by actor and location availability. Sayles envisioned the script as a series of short stories bound together by a common style and score.[64] To ensure continuity, the wardrobe department took a series of polaroids to capture looks in each scene.[65] Similarly, the art department considered both individual sets and the overall aesthetic of the film. They took special care in locating period-specific details, searching through local flea markets for items such as thirty-year-old chewing tobacco that would have been sold in a 1950s café.[66] This attention to detail in creating environments extended even to areas that would not be filmed. For instance, family photographs were added behind the bar at Big O's, creating a unified environment with no possibility for viewer distraction.[67] Larger set pieces were built by the construction department, while the props department provided items to complete each scene's action, "from the tunes in the jukebox to a smoking gun to plates of steaming Mexican food to just the right amount of dust under the wheels of a car or smoke in a busy roadhouse."[68]

Aware of the tight schedule and budgeting concerns, he worked with his producers to maximize efficiency on set, while ensuring a humane working environment for his cast and crew. Sayles frequently carries over crew members from project to project, creating an easy familiarity. While crew members faced challenging weather conditions and other obstacles during filming, producers were sensitive to maintaining reasonable working hours and accommodations.[69] For the cast, Sayles ensured that the actors were familiar with his vision for their characters by providing every cast member a backstory to help explain their character motivations. This was particularly important as Sayles did not conduct rehearsals but wanted to capture "the shock of the new."[70] Nor did the schedule allow room for improvisation.[71] Chris Cooper, whose character backstory begins, "Sam has always lived in reaction to other men and wants to stop," described these backstories as a "great springboard for getting on the same track as [Sayles]."[72] Storyboards sketched out camera angles and character blocking, and detailed scene breakdowns described lighting, mood, and props.

Writer Caroline Hall Otis, who was a college friend of Maggie Renzi's and wanted to learn more about film production, joined the crew as a cable puller and documented her daily impressions of the filming process. Through her diary, Hall Otis was consistently impressed with Sayles's ability to engage in conversation on seemingly any topic (at the cast welcome dinner, they discussed training seals) and for his unusual capacity to give more than one task his full attention at once. Off set, Sayles spent down time playing basketball with the grips and was careful to stay rested, but on set he was fully present. Hall Otis observed, "Our director, John, is always completely himself—calm, focused, engaged, low-key, accessible—he sets the tone for the whole company."[73] Hall Otis continued, "Because John wears the editor hat as well as that of writer and director, he sets up his shots very efficiently, virtually cutting as he goes. John doesn't waste time and he doesn't waste film."[74] Sayles views each of the three roles—writer, director, and editor—as drafts of the final process, each bringing him closer to his desired result.[75] Because he controls the final cut, he is clear when he has seen the take that works for his vision—which could range from between one and fifteen takes to capture a scene. Sayles explains, "I know where I'm going to cut it, and I've got what I need, trust me."[76]

While Sayles is well known for maintaining creative control of his projects, he did consider feedback from his backers. In a letter to Castle Rock executives, Maggie Renzi and Paul Miller reference a recent meeting to discuss the film's rough cut when "John may have seemed intransigent" about Castle Rock's suggestions, but ultimately accepted many of them.[77] Notably, he cut out a scene that was set at Sam's house where, in a fantasy sequence, Sam imagines Buddy killing Wade. As a producer, Renzi did much of the necessary interfacing with the cast, crew, and investors. Observing Sayles and Renzi's working dynamic, Hall Otis concluded, "This is one good personal and creative partnership."[78]

CRITICAL RECEPTION

The first set of viewer responses to *Lone Star* came from test audiences. On March 27, 1996, a recruited audience screening *Lone Star* was held at the Chez Artiste Landmark Theatre in Denver, Colorado, followed by a focus group discussion. The summary concluded that *Lone Star* "did not play well" to this audience, which comprised those between eighteen and thirty-four years old. The audience reported concerns about the length and slow pacing of the film, confusion regarding the multitude of characters and subplots, and a mixed response to Sam and Pilar's concluding plot twist.[79] A press screening held in New York City on May 16, 1996, however, yielded much more favorable feedback, with attendees praising the acting, complex plot line, and the film's beautiful landscape. One representative from a radio station questioned, "Why can't other moviemakers do the things [Sayles] does?" before commenting on the strength of the characters and the "powerful and provocative" story.[80]

While Castle Rock's financing assured that the film would be automatically sold to cable, the broader distribution plans were left open.[81] While it is not common for filmmakers to enter production without an established plan for distribution, Sayles had taken a different approach. After a debut at South by Southwest, he screened *Lone Star* at European film festivals, where he engaged in heavy promotion to raise interest in the film and secure a distribution deal.[82] It opened the Director's Fortnight, an independent sidebar at the famed festival in Cannes, France, where a reviewer declared it the "best of the new American films at Cannes."[83] Sayles held additional screenings at the Cork film festival in Ireland and the Latin Film festival in London. His strategy

Figure 3. Promotional poster of *Lone Star.*

was successful. Sony Picture Classics, an independent division of Sony Pictures Entertainment focused on arthouse and independent films, agreed to manage the release of *Lone Star* in the United States, while Castle Rock handled worldwide distribution.[84] In June 1996, *Lone Star* was released in the US, with a slow rollout in targeted neighborhoods where the film would have clear appeal; a wider release followed.[85] Overall, the film made thirteen million dollars at the box office.

Since its release, film critics, journalists, and scholars have responded to *Lone Star* with a largely positive assessment. The film was widely praised for "some of the most quietly accomplished acting to be found in any recent American movie."[86] Some critics complain the screenplay was overly didactic, with *The Orlando Sentinel* identifying a "liberal pushiness" to the script, noting that "the less politically progressive somebody is, the greater chance that he is corrupt."[87] The British newspaper *The Independent* further critiqued direct speeches that overshadowed the "otherwise understated musings on the weight of history," while a local San Francisco newspaper suggested that Sayles's ability to look at things from multiple angles "is exactly what makes him a muddy filmmaker."[88] However, Robert Ebert, who was one of many critics who placed the film on their top-ten list of films in 1996, wrote, "John Sayles' *Lone Star* contains so many riches, it humbles ordinary movies. And yet they aren't thrown before us, to dazzle and impress: It is only later, thinking about the film, that we appreciate the full reach of its material."[89] *Lone Star* went on to receive numerous nominations and awards, from organizations including the Writers Guild of America, the Texas Film Critics Awards, the NCLR Bravo Awards, the Southeastern Film Critics Association, the Imagen Foundation, and the Film Independent Spirit Awards. The film was also nominated for Best Screenplay at the Golden Globes and for Best Original Screenplay at the Academy Awards. Elizabeth Peña and Ron Canada were singled out for their performances.

For years after the film was released, it was available only as a VHS or DVD. However, in 2024, *Lone Star* was rereleased as a 4K Blu-ray via the Criterion Collection in a package that includes a conversation with Sayles and award-winning American director Gregory Nava, as well as an interview with director of photography Stuart Dryburgh. The inclusion of the film in the Criterion collection, which publishes classic and contemporary films in the highest technical quality, indicates the film's enduring significance.

Several books have been devoted to Sayles's films; additionally available are two books of interviews of Sayles and an unauthorized bibliography, in which *Lone Star* is addressed in parts of chapters.[90] Scholarly writing about *Lone Star* has appeared in book chapters, journal articles, and published lectures. In a scholarly examination of the Western genre, Matthew Carter notes that *Lone Star* "remains the prominent and oft-cited example of transnationalism in the cinematic Western."[91] Additional essays include focused examinations of *Lone Star*'s narrative strategies and depictions of race, class, and sexuality. My study is the first monograph devoted entirely to *Lone Star*.

CONCLUSION

Lone Star anticipates many of today's cultural and political divides, from debates over immigration and border control, to memorialization and public-school curriculum. As a professor, I have included *Lone Star* in my Cinema of the American West course, which I have taught for fifteen years. In this course, I ask my students to consider how the film addresses borderlines (both real and imagined), explores divergent cultural memories, and provides a vision of social change. It is a film I never tire of returning to and one that my students consistently find engaging and relevant. Through his use of live segues and overlapping storytelling, Sayles demonstrates how personal and collective histories continue to resonate in the present day. Characters struggle with the weight of these histories, contemplating whether it is possible to start from scratch—that "blood only means what you let it." Building on Neil Campbell's suggestion that knowing the past is necessary to move on from it, I argue that *Lone Star* calls for a liberation from the past, but not a rejection of it. To show this, I address the film through three major lenses—border crossings, historical memory, and institutional change. In each section, I employ close readings of relevant scenes to show how *Lone Star* develops frameworks for pursuing personal, cultural, and institutional liberation, and therefore, creates new stories for the future.

1. | Border Crossings

Lone Star presents Hispanic, African American, Anglo, and Native American histories in the US/Mexico borderlands as deeply intertwined, contentious, and ongoing. Over the course of the film, borders break down between time, space, and people, demonstrating the liberatory possibilities of border crossing. However, *Lone Star* also recognizes the practical, legal, and ethical restrictions of living with imposed borders. On a personal level, Sayles reflects that a border exists where a line is drawn that indicates "This is where I end and somebody else begins. In a metaphorical sense, it can be any of the symbols we erect against each other—sex, class, race, age."[1] Broadly, borders create what one character refers to as "lines of demarcation" between cultural groups, closing off communication. When this occurs, Sayles observes, it becomes easier for each side to mythologize the other and, in turn, to view them as an enemy. As a result, stories of conflict and violence pervade the borderlands.

In *The Multi-Cultural Southwest: A Reader*, the editors liken the American Southwest to an ancient map on which lines have been continuously drawn and redrawn to tell the stories of "migrations, conquests, rebellion, settlements, trails, and boom-and-bust enterprises."[2]

This region has held multiple identities as "the Azlan of Aztec mythology, the Seven Cities of Cibola of the Spanish Empire, Mexico's buffer against American expansion, and America's frontier."[3] It can be understood as a contact zone, a phrase famously employed by anthropologist Mary Louise Pratt to describe "social spaces where cultures meet, clash, and grapple with each other, often in contexts of highly asymmetrical relations of power."[4] In addition to these internal struggles, the borderland region consistently remains on the periphery of empire, rather than a locus of power.

The United States shares a nearly two thousand-mile international border with Mexico, another line that has been drawn and redrawn. Following the battle of the Alamo, and the capture of Santa Anna later in 1836, Texas became a republic. In 1846, the US invaded Mexico, which resulted in the capture of land that encompassed present-day Texas, New Mexico, Arizona, Colorado, and California, and moved the border south a hundred miles to the Rio Grande. Pricilla Solis Ybarra comments that because of the Mexican-American War "approximately one hundred thousand Mexicans, without moving an inch, suddenly found themselves residing within U.S. boundaries" where they faced dispossession of their lands.[5] Contemporary immigration rights activists have referenced this land loss with their rallying call, "We didn't cross the border, the border crossed us."[6]

The current border was established in 1848 with the signing of the Treaty of Guadalupe-Hidalgo.[7] A natural marker covering hundreds of miles, the changing course of the Rio Grande throughout the nineteenth and twentieth centuries led to international disagreements.[8] Erosion and flooding created new channels, turning operating farmland into a contested international boundary, causing man-made attempts to redivert the river to maintain the boundary.[9] For instance, an area of Mexican farmland known as Chamizal was bisected by the shifting river, while the nearby Cordova Island encroached on El Paso, creating a land dispute lasting nearly a century. In 1962, US President John F. Kennedy and Mexican President Adolfo Lopez Mateos collaborated to build a concrete lined channel for the Rio Grande to divide the two areas, which was completed in 1968. As a result, more than five thousand residents with Mexican citizenship were forced to relocate south to comply with the new international border.[10]

Because Mexican immigration does not require crossing an ocean, Western historian Patricia Nelson Limerick writes, "the relationship between immigrant and home country is thus substantially different from other forms of U.S. immigration."[11] Sayles's recognition that this international border has shifted over time, and can seem arbitrary in nature, carries over into *Lone Star*. In addition to his early travels in Texas that disrupted his notion of neat separations between cultures, Sayles was during filming further struck by the artificiality of the border. He said, "When we were in any of those border towns, one of the things you realize is the majority of the people speak Spanish at home on the Anglo side as well as the Mexican side. They have cousins and friends on the other side. The governments are the people who are separating them."[12] In *Lone Star*, however, borders between people and places exist in flux.

Sayles's representation of the borderlands aligns with scholarly reexaminations of the American West in the 1980s and 1990s. In *Borderlands/La Frontera: The New Mestiza*, published in 1987, Chicana poet and activist Gloria Anzaldúa employs the visceral and oft-cited metaphor that the US/Mexico border is an open wound "where the Third

World grates against the first and bleeds." As a result of this friction, a third country—a border culture—emerges.[13] Like *Lone Star*, Anzaldúa's text addresses both the geopolitical border and other forms of cultural, class, gender, and psychological borders.[14] A border, she writes, is a "dividing line, a narrow strip along a steep edge. A borderland is a vague and undetermined place created by the emotional residue of an unnatural boundary. It is in a constant state of transition."[15] However, the complexities of the region have been simplified in official historical narratives.

Historians of the American West were long influenced by Frederick Jackson Turner's 1893 Frontier Thesis, which suggested that westward expansion, along an expanding frontier line, shaped an exceptional American national character, which centered on the rugged individualism of white men. This historical idea of frontier, with its emphasis on American innocence and exceptionalism, has become entrenched in popular culture, carrying a "persistently happy affect, a tone of adventure, heroism, and even fun very much in contrast with the tough, complicated, and sometimes bloody and brutal realities of conquest."[16] This sanitized popular culture of the frontier emerged from folktales, popular writing, and live performances, highlighting Manifest Destiny and progressivism.[17] From the late nineteenth century, artists such as Albert Bierstadt, Charles M. Russell, and Frederic Remington painted idealized depictions of the American West, creating a mythic vision that directly continued in the realm of cinema. In the twentieth century, filmmakers such as John Ford crafted films that flowed from this "vibrant tradition in the visual arts."[18] In the 1960s, this vision began to fracture, as American social divisions increased during the Vietnam War and civil rights movement, which led to "alternative images of a more pluralistic American society and culture."[19] Some historians of the West began to advocate for a redefinition of the frontier as "a contested zone of cross-cultural meetings."[20]

Beginning in the 1980s, the "new western history" movement more forcefully sought alternatives to the Frontier Thesis, as key scholars such as Limerick, William Cronon, Richard White, and Donald Worster highlighted previously silenced voices and considered issues of race, class, gender, and the environment. Building on Anzaldúa's 1994 essay "The Adventures of the Frontier Myth in the Twentieth Century," Limerick argued for the model of la frontera, a "much less familiar but much more realistic" understanding of the borderlands between the United States and Mexico that includes "borders between countries, between peoples, between authorities."[21] La frontera is a geographic and metaphorical borderland that resists the linearity of the frontier line and instead embraces the cultural and moral complexity of the American West. She proposes that "If *la frontera* had anywhere near the standing of the idea of the frontier, we would be well launched toward self-understanding, directed toward a realistic view of this nation's position in the hemisphere and in the world."[22] Given the longevity of the frontier fantasy in popular culture, Limerick projected her hope that by the mid-2000s popular culture would move toward the reality of *la frontera* and "begin to reckon with the complexity of western movement and its consequences."[23]

Well ahead of Limerick's predicted timeline, *Lone Star*'s fictional town of Frontera provides an embodiment of la frontera, visualizing the past and present as a continuum and demonstrating the social, political, and economic struggles that result from the region's complex multicultural history. Perhaps most significant for *Lone Star* is that, as

Figure 4. Big O's.

Kimberly Sultze remarks, "La frontera is conceived as a running story, not as a neatly corralled model with a clear beginning and end in time (history) or in space (geography), nor with a simple solitary direction of movement east to west."[24] Both the film's live segues through time and the dialogue itself reinforce the theme of border crossing. Neil Campbell further observes that characters in *Lone Star* are "perpetually engaged with the consequences of living amid centuries of 'intercultural crossing and mixing.'" This active grappling with complex histories prompts the rethinking of frontier frameworks that insist upon discreet "territorial identities, separated lives, and unrelated histories."[25]

In *Lone Star*, the town of Frontera is divided spatially into "the separate parts where the Anglos, the Mexicans, and the Indians live, Fort Mackenzie (which is soon to be closed), and Darktown."[26] Cinematographer Stuart Dryburgh imagined each character operating within that character's own world, with Frontera operating as a "collection of little worlds, of worlds colliding."[27] As these worlds collide, they are shown to be less separate than they appear. This chapter considers the misunderstandings, struggles, and shifts in authority that occur when people cross borders. Key scenes for discussion include Otis's exhibition of Black Seminoles, Sam's trip to Mexico to investigate the murder of Eladio Cruz, and Mercedes's encounter with migrants crossing the Rio Grande near her Frontera home. *Lone Star* suggests that borderlines are often blurry, subjective, and open to negotiation.

BLACK SEMINOLE MUSEUM

When Delmore Payne returned to Frontera to command the soon-to-close Fort McKenzie, his son Chet was curious to learn more about the grandfather he had never met. Otis Payne is known as the "Mayor of Darktown," and his club, Big O's, is a gathering place for Frontera's small African American community. Viewers are introduced to the club during a brief exterior shot that has Chet peering through a front window. As he enters, club lights flash, arguments and laughter erupt from the crowd, and Little Walter's "Boogie" blares from the jukebox. The camera focuses on Chet's moving through the crowd, purposely walking forward toward Otis as his hand slowly reaches into his jacket pocket. Their relationship has not yet been established, and Chet's approach feels slightly ominous. However, the scene subverts expectations when Chet only reaches for an advertisement for "Big O's South Texas Barbeque Sauce"; only then does a shot ring out from the back of the club. Otis quickly spots Chet and ushers him out, noting firmly, "You weren't in here tonight, were you?"

Figure 5. Otis escorts Chet out of Big O's.

This shooting, which involved an army private, sets the stage for Delmore, Otis's estranged son, to pay an "official visit" to the roadhouse to investigate. While the visit is meant to help determine whether to restrict access to the club, it reconnects Delmore with his father for the first time since his return to Frontera. In explaining the importance of Big O's as an outlet for the Black community on base, Otis describes the club and a local church as the only places where Black people in Frontera feel truly comfortable. Beyond its normal operations, Otis sees the bar as a place where people can find needed help—a place to stay, a loan—and connection. In defending his patrons, Otis reflects his belief in human complexity noting, "It's not like there is a borderline between

Figure 6. Delmore pays Otis an official visit.

the good people and the bad people." Delmore, an Army Colonel tasked with enforcing a high level of order and rigidity, has no inclination to accept this expansive perspective. When Otis asks to meet his family, Delmore hesitates, and then responds vaguely, "You'll get my official notification when I make my decision," which may be a response to either the investigation or Otis's request.[28]

Otis's view of flexible borders is further explored when Chet returns to Big O's and discovers his grandfather's Black Seminole Museum in the back of his club. Before Chet enters, an exterior shot of the roadhouse reveals a bleached white exterior, picnic tables, and a handmade sign for the museum. Inside, Chet discovers that his grandfather, known for his award-winning barbeque sauce, also serves as a local historian. In his museum, Otis has compiled documentation and artistic renderings of his ancestors, who as runaway slaves escaped to the Florida Everglades and joined up with the Seminole Indians.[29] Through intermarriage, their mixed-race descendants were subject to Indian removal, when the Seminole were forcibly displaced to western lands.[30] Otis's museum features drawings of one of these descendants, John Horse—or in Spanish, Juan Caballo—who was famed for resisting removal for over a decade before crossing the border to Mexico to fight with General Santa Anna's armies. Looking at this image, Chet questions, "Was he a black man or an Indian?" Otis explains that he was "both." Horse and his fighting band eventually entered Texas and became scouts of the US Army, who, Otis notes, were the "best trackers on either side of the border." The Black Seminoles were tasked with tracking down other Indians, an act that stuns Chet. Tomás Sandoval notes that through this encounter, Chet is presented with "a hybrid mix of escaped slaves and Native Americans whose 'border' identities reveal notions of origin or essence inadequate."[31] Mary Helen Washington further comments, "These multiple identities that Big O narrates seem to keep multiplying. And there is no attempt to evade the problematics of the history of black Indians fighting other Indians on the side of a colonizing army."[32]

Chet, who was shown to be visibly bored in Pilar's history class, is suddenly engaged as he absorbs what this information means to his own identity. He questions, "So, I'm part Indian?" In response, Otis again deflects the notion of fixed identities, noting that "By blood you are. But blood only means what you let it." Chet responds to this comment with the philosophy his father has raised him with: "From the day you're born you start from scratch. No breaks. No excuses. You got to pull yourself up on your own." This belief, likely stemming from Delmore's estrangement with Otis, suggests that the past is a detriment to future progress. In writing this scene, Sayles acknowledges that it is impossible to start from scratch: "Nobody does that. Everybody starts with some kind of handicap or advantage, and that's their personal history. And it's also their group history."[33] However, Sayles was interested in exploring the extent to which people are expected to be responsible for themselves regardless of their pasts.

While this scene depicts a broader history of African American, Native American, and Mexican engagement in the borderland, Chet is also learning his own history for the first time.[34] From Celie's visit with Pilar, we learn that Chet has most recently attended school on a military base in Korea and has likely moved many times in his life. By returning to Frontera, he experiences the possibility of connecting with his family and history. However, when Otis tells Chet that "blood only means what you let it," he is suggesting that people are not defined by their history and that Chet can choose the aspects of his own heritage that he wishes to embrace. While Delmore has firmly closed off his own past, Sandoval writes, "In his own way, Otis asserts choice, self-determination and rejects the mastery of history to define our lives."[35] Through this first visit with his grandfather, Chet begins to understand the complexity and divisions within his immediate family, as well as his ancestors. Sandoval continues, "Celebrating Black Seminole heroes of the past, the museum's artifacts tell the history that continues to live in the present through that base, Otis, and his grandson."[36]

SAM'S BORDER CROSSING

Otis's narrative about John Horse tells a story about racial borderlines, as well as geographic border crossings. In *Lone Star*, characters cross this geopolitical border in multiple ways. Sam's investigation into his father's potential misdeeds, Washington writes, "involve many border crossings, some literal, some psychological and metaphorical, and each border crossing requires the relinquishing of power."[37] Sam's travel to Mexico requires him to set aside his authority as a sheriff as he experiences a shift in both geography and his understanding of the past.

After hearing the custodian at his office accuse Charlie Wade of murdering Eladio Cruz, Sam decides to drive across the border to visit Chucho Montoya, a witness of the murder. (This leads to a humorous exchange when he mentions to his colleague Ray that he is "going over to the other side" and Ray, confused, responds "The Republicans?") Leaving his conversation with Ray, he removes his sheriff's badge and by doing that signals he understands his jurisdiction as sheriff ends at the border. Sam drives on a highway toward the large "Welcome to Mexico" sign, posted in both English and Spanish, that greets travelers crossing into Ciudad Juárez by car and foot. Spanish-language music plays as he leaves behind a nondescript landscape of hotels and McDonalds signs. Entering Mexico, the camera cuts to colorful taco stands and a bronze bust of Benito Juarez with the word "reform" visible under his torso.

The music on the radio transitions to an advertisement for Chucho Montoya's tire shop. As he drives, Sam passes Anselma, Enrique's fiancé, who stands in front of a small market and turns her head to watch him pass. When the scene cuts to the *llantería* (tire shop), Sam immediately enters into conversation with Montoya, the self-proclaimed "El Rey de las Llantas" or "King of Tires," who owns a string of shops in Ciudad

Leon that use recycled parts. He tells Sam, "A lot of your people rolling over that bridge on my rubber." Sam briefly questions Montoya about his time in the United States, before casually asking, "Hey, you ever know a fella named Eladio Cruz?"

The question provokes an extended dialogue between the two in which Montoya points out Sam's lack of authority on this side of the border.

Montoya: You're the sheriff of Rio County, right? Un jefe muy respetado [a highly respected chief].

[Montoya leans over to draw a line in the dirt with his Coke bottle.]

Step across this line.

[Sam complies.]

Ay, qué milagro! [Oh, what a miracle!] You're not the sheriff of nothing anymore. Just some Tejano with a lot of questions I don't have to answer. A bird flying south—you think he sees this line? Rattlesnake, javelina—whatever you got. You think halfway across that line they start thinking different? Why should a man?

Sam: Your government's been pretty happy to have that line. The question's just been where to draw it—

Montoya: My government can go fuck itself and so can yours. I'm talking about people here. Men. Mi amigo, Eladio Cruz—is giving his friends a lift one day in his camión [truck]. But since they're on one side of this invisible line and not the other, they got to hide in the back, como criminales. And because over there, he's just another Mex bracero [laborer] . . . any man with a badge is his jefe.

Figure 7. Chucho Montoya draws a line in the dirt.

The actor who played Montoya, Tony Amendola, had the idea of using the Coke bottle, emblematic of American corporate culture, as his tool for drawing a line in the dirt. But that same line alludes more distantly to the story of the Alamo, to the time when Colonel William Travis famously took his sword to draw a line in the sand, offering anyone who wanted to leave to cross over.[38]

Montoya also affirms what Sam understood in removing his badge—that in Mexico he is "not the sheriff of nothing anymore." That same loss of authority in crossing borders also figures in Welles's *Touch of Evil,* as Mexican drug enforcement agent Miguel Vargas (Charlton Heston) is forced to work with American police captain Hank Quinlan (Welles) in investigating a car bomb explosion at the border. Likewise, in the 2013 series *The Bridge*, Detective Sonya Cross (Diane Kruger) from the El Paso Police Department must collaborate with Chihuahua State Police Detective Marco Ruiz (Demián Bichir) to solve the crime of two female bodies melded together and placed on the Bridge of the Americas. Cross's supervisor, Lt. Hank Wade, warns her that a task force would be necessary as their case would take them to Mexico, "and last I checked that badge on your hip don't mean shit in Juarez." This "relinquishing of power," which Washington captures, describes perfectly what Sam must accept when he, too, crosses the border into Mexico.

As Montoya speaks, he turns to his side. As he does, the camera pans left across his tire advertisement and across the landscape back to 1956, where a truck is broken down on a bridge that spans a large arroyo. The truck belongs to Eladio Cruz, a Frontera native, who works in construction and farm labor north of the border and, with his friend Chucho, supplements his income by smuggling illegal laborers into Texas for their white employer.[39] As Eladio changes the tire, to his dismay a young Chucho leaves his hiding spot in the back of the truck to relieve himself under the bridge. From this vantage point, Chucho sees Charley Wade approaching in his car marked Rio County Sheriff; Hollis trails behind, and Spanish-language music sets the scene. Wade and Cruz exchange greetings in Spanish before Wade questions him about what he is hauling in his truck. While Cruz claims he is taking watermelons to the market, Wade pushes, "I heard somebody's been hauling wets on this road .... That person's been bragging all over the county how he doesn't have to cut that gringo sheriff in on it. Run his own operation without any help." After asking Cruz for his name, he asks whether he is carrying a firearm for protection. When Cruz replies, "just a shotgun" and leans to get it, Wade shoots him twice in the back, killing him. He continues

Figure 8. Charley Wade shoots Eladio Cruz.

his tirade unfazed, "Little greaser son of a bitch is running a goddam bus service. Thinks he can make a fool out of Charley Wade." While Wade calls for Hollis's help to examine the back of the truck, Hollis is frozen in horror, finally managing to weakly exclaim, "You killed him!" Wade replies, "You got a talent for stating the obvious, son."

The camera cuts back to Chucho crouched under the bridge, who has witnessed his friend's murder, but was unable to take any kind of action to change it. Sulze writes that this scene demonstrates "the inhumane actions that can occur on one side or on the other because of our lines."[40] Prior to the murder, the good-humored Chucho spent much of his life crossing back and forth over the border, between family on both sides, and "playing its angles for what he can get."[41] Seeing his best friend unjustly killed fills him with a sense of bitterness that his decades as a successful business owner never quite alleviated. Here, his backstory helps: "The Border that he looks at every day is a constant symbol of what is unfair in life, and though he accepts unfairness as a fact, he will never be resigned to it."[42] The scene turns from young Chucho, as he hears footsteps above. The camera pans upward, this time with the footsteps belonging to a present-day Sam, who approaches to peer over the same bridge. While Chucho at first appears reluctant to speak with Sam, he unburdens himself by sharing his testimony of eyewitnessing Eladio's death.

MERCEDES'S BORDER CROSSING

Sam's border crossing occurs at an international bridge, and he is freely admitted to Mexico and back. A flashback reveals that for young Mercedes entering the United States involved a treacherous crossing of the Rio Grande. Once she crossed this border, she never returned to Mexico. Sayles's backstory for Mercedes reads:

> Mercedes embodies all the conflicts of a border town. She came up from the interior of Mexico in her mid-teens at great personal risk because there was no future for her in the town she grew up in. Her father spoke Spanish and her mother spoke an Indian language, and there was prejudice against her even in her native country.[43]

Initially Mercedes Cruz seems to exemplify the "start from scratch" mentality espoused by Delmore. She denies her own roots and experiences to fully assimilate into the United States. Deeply established in Frontera, Mercedes runs the successful Santa Barbara Cafe and serves

Figure 9. Pilar talks with Mercedes at the café.

as a member of City of Council. At the memorial unveiling for Buddy, Hollis describes her as "one of Frontera's most prominent citizens."

Mercedes's sharp feelings about the recent migrants she employs in her restaurant is apparent in a scene when Pilar visits her at the café. The camera follows them as Mercedes moves through the busy kitchen, scolding employees who are helping with prep, to the sounds of sizzling food and clinking dishes. Mercedes's frustrations boil over, repeatedly reminding her employees to "speak English!" and at one point exclaiming "these people are stealing from me!" However, when Pilar critiques her for hiring illegal immigrants, Mercedes becomes defensive, insisting that all her employees have green cards and that she is following the law. In the same scene, Mercedes shows little interest in engaging her own history. When Pilar asks her mother whether she would be interested in accompanying her and her son Amado (who, Pilar explains, is on a big "Tejano roots" kick) down south to see where Mercedes grew up, Mercedes replies, "You want to see Mexicans? Open your eyes and look around you. We're up to our ears in them."[44]

In a later scene at the school where Mercedes is absent, Pilar provides insight to her mother's attitude about race. When her colleague Marisol encourages Pilar to discuss her romantic interests, referring to one potential partner as being drawn to "hot-blooded Mexican girls," Pilar quickly interrupts, "Spanish, please. My mother would have a heart attack." When Marisol questions whether her mother's family is Spanish, Pilar sarcastically responds, "They go back to Cortez. When he was riding by, they were squatting in a hut cooking hamsters for dinner." When her colleague insists that she pay attention to her love life because all Pilar does is work, Pilar replies, "All my mother does is work. It's how you get to be Spanish." Marisol refers, tongue-in-cheek, to a stereotype of sexually precocious "Mexican girls," entrenched in popular culture, and who date back to nineteenth-century dime novels. Sam Hall's 1886 *Little Lone Star*, for instance, features a young Mexican woman living in Texas whose passions are comparable to "the red-hot volcanoes of her Native Mexico," who becomes the love interest of an Anglo-Texan cowboy.[45] Such love matches, as later demonstrated in Fred Zinneman's *High Noon* (1952), are rarely shown to work out, which is in keeping with broader cultural expectations.

When Pilar interjects that her mother claims Spanish ancestry, she is referring to a strategic identity with layered historical implications.[46] In the late nineteenth and early twentieth centuries, such claims emphasized European heritage to create distance from negative Mexican stereotypes.[47] This reinforced what, in 1948, Carey McWilliams called a Southwest "fantasy heritage," which denied ethnic intermingling and lauded Spanish colonizers as heroes.[48] For Mercedes, distancing herself from Indigenous and Mexican ancestry is another way she tries to separate herself from her personal history. However, this disconnect is not absolute. Through her business, she provides Mexican food and music to the community.

Her feelings about her background are further complicated by the reveal that her husband Eladio was killed while helping others cross the border. Her backstory proves informative as she was always worried early in her marriage about Eladio's smuggling activities; she also believed that Frontera's Mexican and Mexican American majority would eventually lead to more social power and opportunity. The loss of her husband, in addition, also unmoored and hardened her.[49] While she shows an extreme commitment to hard work and proclaims to Pilar that she never wanted "some chulo with grease under his nails drinking up the profits," we later learn that Mercedes was financially assisted by Buddy in establishing her business. Eventually she and Buddy entered a long-term affair, quietly tolerated by the community, that led to the birth of Pilar. While Mercedes's later disapproval of Sam and Pilar's romance drove a wedge between her and her daughter, Mercedes maintained a quiet loyalty to Buddy over the years, which her deciding vote to name the memorial courthouse in his honor confirmed.

Her personal history of entering the United States is unveiled through her encounter with her employee, Enrique, who, she discovers, helps other migrants cross the Rio Grande. Her approach to illegal crossings is made clear early in the film. As Mercedes relaxes on her porch by the river one evening, she eagerly calls Border Patrol on unnamed migrants stealing through the dark. However, when her Enrique approaches her after his fiancé is injured in an attempted river crossing, she reluctantly becomes invested. Enrique calls out to her on

Figure 10. Unnamed migrants pass Mercedes's home.

her porch, addressing her as "Senora Cruz." After her initial shock of seeing her employee emerge from the darkness, she quickly recovers to remind him to address her "In English. We're in the United States." As Enrique explains that there has been an accident in the river, Mercedes quickly understands what has happened. After she suggests she will call Border Patrol for assistance, despite the pleas that she not do that, she dismissively questions: "You think you're doing these people a favor? What are they going to do? They get on welfare, or they become criminals." Enrique protests, explaining that the injured woman is the mother of his child, even though he married a friend's cousin to live in the United States. Mercedes scoffs, "Typical."

A following scene returns to the Rio Grande. The river is shown to be particularly turbulent, aided by a handheld camera used to film as deep into the river as possible.[50] This time, a young Mercedes is shown in the river alone, yelling out in Spanish, "Where are you? I'm lost! I can't see the bank!" A voice responds from the riverbank, and Mercedes turns toward a man carrying a lantern. Assuring her that her friend has been retrieved, he wades into the water, extending his hand in introduction. Mercedes identifies herself as Mercedes Gonzales Ruiz, he smiles and says "*Me llamo* Eladio Cruz. Bienvenido a Texas."

The camera pans right from their locked hands to the dark rushing water and into present day with Mercedes sternly rushing Enrique and his injured partner to her car to take them to a doctor who had practiced "on the other side" and owes her a few favors. Even though she ultimately decides to help the young couple, she still expresses fear of being caught and takes the time to again scold, "In English, Enrique. In English!" However, our having learned that Mercedes had herself arrived in the country via river crossing decades earlier casts her decision to help the couple in a different light.

Her rigidity in calling border control, insisting on legal processes, and demanding the English language can now be read as hypocritical—her insistence on following a rule that she herself once violated. However, Mercedes has largely buried her memories of the young girl who fell in love with Eladio so many decades ago. She has now cast herself as a model for the community to follow but, in the process, has become very isolated. Sayles writes, "She has paid so much for what she has gotten in this world, it is so tied to painful memories, that she is stuck in a trap of her own making."[51]

Like Delmore, Mercedes firmly shuts out her painful past and has dedicated herself to assimilating into the United States. As Lisa Lowe argues, the process of becoming part of a new nation requires the "forgetting" of personal histories. To engage in the "melting pot" of American identity, racial and ethnic identities must implicitly be left behind. US national culture, in that regard, demands that diverse people and social spaces come together into a unified "whole." For our legal and political forms to function, the individual must identify with this national project. However, as Lowe argues, national culture overshadows inequalities based on race, national origin, and class. Such inequalities must be set aside to accept the "collectively forged images, histories, and narratives that place, displace, and replace individuals in relation to the national polity."[52] Engagement with national culture requires a break with the past. Individual and groups histories must be replaced by the national narrative, which dictates what is remembered and what is forgotten. But as Sandoval points out, and Mercedes experiences, it is not possible to fully escape the weight of the past—"the persistence of race and racism within national discourse illustrates the belief that blood has concrete and inflexible meanings."[53]

However, in helping Enrique and Anselma, Mercedes experiences a "psychological and emotional release" that comes from abandoning "assimilationist ideas and accept the challenge to embrace . . . racial and ethnic histories long suppressed or denied."[54] Mercedes, who has never returned to the riverbank in all of her years in Frontera, is confronted with her painful memories and is able to show new empathy for a new generation facing the same challenges that she once did. The "embodied conflicts" of the borderlands that Mercedes represents for Sayles show that not all Mexicans living along the border are aligned, politically or socially.[55]

THE WESTERN GENRE AND THE CONTEMPORARY BORDER

Again, much of *Lone Star* was shot in Eagle Pass, Texas—just across the border from its sister city, Piedras Negras, Mexico. Eagle Pass was established in 1849 thanks to the establishment of Fort Duncan, a waypoint for Santa Anna and his army on their journey to the Alamo. At the time *Lone Star* was being filmed, Sayles witnessed the local border as a permeable site, easily traversed. He recalled, "While we were there, you could put a dime in a slot and walk through the turnstile and then go have a margarita in Mexico. Or do the opposite and go to Walmart, and then two hours later, back over."[56] During filming, both cast and crew members crossed the border to attend the midnight rodeo disco in Piedras Negras. Cable-puller Caroline Hall Otis recalls running into Matthew McConaughey there, noting that "he knows his way around a cowboy hat."[57] In addition to these social border crossings, the crew worked with border patrol to film scenes in Mexico.

The southern border states have served as a key locale in the Western genre. Marine Soubeille writes that even though in many classic Westerns "the border with Mexico is seen as another frontier where Mexicans stand in for savagery in their Turnerian opposition to Anglo-American culture," this dichotomy has been challenged in films throughout the genre's history.[58] From classic Westerns such as *The Magnificent Seven* (John Sturges, 1960), to spaghetti Westerns such as *A Fistful of Dollars* (Sergio Leone, 1964), to revisionist Westerns such as *The Wild Bunch* (Sam Peckinpah, 1969), varied treatments of the US/Mexico border have provided lenses for understanding US nationhood and transnational engagement.

Historian Richard Slotkin, for one, reads *The Magnificent Seven* as an allegory for American intervention in Vietnam. Both the film and American policy, he argues, address "the same ideologically loaded images of heroism and savagery, the same narrow and essentially racist views of non-White peoples and cultures, and the same hope that all problems can be solved by a burst of action and a spectacular display of massive yet miraculously selective firepower."[59] In the film, a western remake of Akira Kurosawa's *Seven Samurai* (1954), American gunfighters are called on to save a small Mexican farming village from a group of bandits. The offered compensation is minimal, but the gunfighters agree to the work because the western towns they once commanded are now settled, and their only opportunity to continue their lifestyle is by crossing the border. Once they have saved the villagers, the surviving gunfighters must either return to United States or ride on in pursuit of other adventures. In this film, US intervention is framed as morally necessary and paternalistic in nature.

A Fistful of Dollars, an unauthorized remake of Kurasawa's *Yojimbo* (1961), featured an Italian director (Leone), an American star (Clint Eastwood), a Spanish filming location resembling the US/Mexico borderlands, and received German financial backing. After its release in Italy, it was rereleased in the United States in 1967 and helped launch the popularity of spaghetti Westerns, low-budget, Italian-made westerns, that have come to be associated with Leone's distinct style. With bleak landscapes, a discordant score by Ennio Morricone, off-kilter cinematography, and a mysterious leading man with no name or backstory, *A Fistful of Dollars* depicts border crossing as purely transactional, as the man plays upon dueling families to increase his bounty and to position himself opportunistically to play two countries against each other. *The*

Wild Bunch also creates a similarly "amoral and disordered universe," where "civilized" social orders, in both the United States and Mexico, are shown to be deeply flawed. *Bunch* accordingly depicts "heroic alternatives to a fallen civilization that the Western has celebrated: the cavalry troop, the social bandit gang, the chivalric rescuer of women." These films reflect international influence in their production, settings, and themes, as well as demonstrate the expanding borders of the Western genre.

In the twenty-first century, the Western genre has further evolved to reflect the new realities of the border. In *Lone Star*'s original script, Sayles had a small role as a US Federal Border Guard that he later cut from the film. To prepare, he had conversations with local border patrol. At the time, the agents would check to be sure that illegal border crossers from Mexico were not wanted for a crime and then wave them through.[60] They told Sayles that their most common phrase was "don't make me run." In reflecting on *Lone Star* in 2024, when the Criterion Collection version was released, Sayles noted that border patrol agents now face far different realities. For instance, he observed that narcotics traffic has "moved down the border from Laredo and El Paso to all of those towns," and the border patrol is now outfitted in body armor.[61] Border crossers, moreover, are now arriving in greater numbers from Central America's Northern Triangle countries of Honduras, Guatemala, and El Salvador, spurred by violence and climate change. Mexican American film director Gregory Nava, who interviewed Sayles as a special feature on the Criterion release, notably depicted border crossing in *El Norte* (1983), which follows a brother and sister making the dangerous trip from Guatemala to Los Angeles after their family is killed in a government massacre.

Lone Star served as inspiration for other transnational Westerns that also explore the complexity of the borderlands. The film *The Three Burials of Melquiades Estrada* (2005), directed by and starring Tommy Lee Jones, takes this approach. After border officer Mike Norton (Barry Pepper) wrongfully kills and covers up the death of Mexican ranch hand Melquiades Estrada (Julio Cesar Cedillo), his friend and employer in Texas, Pete Perkins (Jones), travels across the border with Estrada's corpse to give him a proper burial in his hometown. This film, written by Guillermo Arriaga, addresses the imposition of an international border running through the center of a culture, as well as the violence of the border patrol in confronting "border jumpers." Matthew Carter argues that, like *Lone Star, Three Burials* is an important addition to the realization of la frontera in popular culture. The film depicts "the borderlands as an in-between space, one that is not simply defined as a line drawn between two distinct and wholly different countries, societies, cultures. Instead, it is depicted as a space with its own character and meaning, one that is inseparable from history and myth."[62] Jones includes dialogue in both Spanish and English and employs a narrative structure marked by a distinctive "temporal and spatial disjuncture," moving between past and present to slowly explain the relationship between Pete and Melquiades.[63]

Other contemporary Western films retain this complexity, while focusing on the new realities of heightened border security, warring cartels, and increased narcotics activity, among others.[64] These Westerns, Campbell writes, "chart a complex and varied response to a changing cultural, economic, and political landscape and, in so doing, help to diagnose and interrogate the multiple dimensions of the American post-West."[65] For example, the critically acclaimed *No Country for Old Men* (2007), directed by Joel and Ethan Coen, is centered on an illicit drug deal gone wrong. Set in the "tense, fuzzy borderland" of West Texas (with Las Vegas, Nevada, standing in for Eagle Pass in filming), the opening scene features bodies scattered in the desert, its "trucks, guns, drugs, and bullet casings all echo[ing] the sheriff's star, skull, and bullets that haunt *Lone Star*."[66] While 2015's *Sicario*, directed by Denis Villeneuve, focuses on an escalating drug war in an Arizona border town, Soubeille argues that this film reverts to a more simplistic division and separation of cultures.[67] In contrast, the independent film *Tejano* (2018), directed by David Blue Garcia, which parodies Western conventions in telling the story of a Tejano farmer-turned-drug smuggler, follows films like *Lone Star* and *Three Burials* in translating la frontera to film.

Beyond the impact of narcotics traffic, Sales suggests that the "symbolic weight and literal weight" of the border wall would need to be included if he were making *Lone Star* today.[68] He explains, "The symbol of the wall has gotten so important to certain people in politics and certain voters who support those people that it means more, and it's allowed to stand between these people who would be pretty happy to just co-exist."[69] In a recent interview, Chris Cooper praised Sayles for his storytelling being "[twenty] years ahead of his time," noting that the border conflict today is a "nightmare." However, Cooper states that *Lone Star* effectively shows that history is never too far away from the present day and that the issues at the border will take many years to resolve, if ever. In the meantime, Sayles reflects, "I don't think a wall is the answer: it's like a Christo installation that has cost billions of dollars. I recently visited it with a friend, and we urinated on it."[70]

While the US/Mexico border is fraught with new pressures and populations of border crossers, this basic desire to coexist remains potent. The 2015 documentary *Western*, directed by filmmakers Bill and Turner Ross, focuses on the border area of Eagle Pass and Piedras Negras and follows two characters, "a cowboy and a lawman." The cowboy is cattle broker Martín Wall, a Texas rancher who procures cattle in Mexico and sells them on the American market, and the lawman is Chad Foster, the then-mayor of Eagle Pass, who is described as a "champion of the region's shared history and culture." The film opens as the bilingual Foster hosts a parade honoring this shared heritage. *Western* reflects well-known traditions of the West Texas border culture against reports of recent gang murders and drug violence that have cast a shadow on daily life.

While the Western genre has continued to expand its borders to incorporate new stories and experiences, in *Lone Star* border crossings are similarly generative—of new relations, new institutions, and new possibilities. Sayles has said of his characters, "I want them to cross the border. We're meeting these people as human beings with their own problems and how they meet these rules. When people can get around, things can be better. There are a lot of things we have in common."[71]

2. | Historical Memory

In *Lone Star,* memories, both personal and collective, are transferred across generations. In *Tangled Memories,* Marita Sturken states that cultural memory—the way a specific culture engages in collective remembrance—differs from personal memory and history.[1] Where individual memory is fragmentary and incomplete, cultural memory steps in to fill the gaps. In the process of collective remembering, certain choices are made about what gets remembered and forgotten. Therefore, when individual memories are conjured, they can create sites of opposition within cultural memory. *Lone Star* directly addresses the tangled nature of history and memory. The dialogue-heavy script shows that memory operates as a narrative, existing only in its telling, rather than as a replica of experience. Memory is, in addition, fallible and subject to the interests of the teller, which can lead to conflicts over how to view the past. History, therefore, is not fully stable or contained, as it always spills over into the present. The historical debates represented in *Lone Star* remain relevant nearly thirty years after its release, as memorials of colonizers and Confederate leaders are removed across the country, and, as I consider in chapter 3, school curriculums serve as political battlegrounds.

Lone Star opens with an exhumation of the past. While Western genre conventions often include an opening shot that establishes a mythic landscape, *Lone Star* begins at ground level, panning across a desert scrub landscape.[2] In the foreground, a man consults a guidebook to identify local plants, while another uses a metal detector in the

Figure 11. Sam examines Wade's sheriff's badge.

distance. The men, Cliff Hogan and Mikey Potts, are sergeants exploring an abandoned rifle range near the army base on their day off and soon make a major discovery in the dirt—a half-buried skull, sheriff's badge, and mason ring. Frontera's current sheriff, Sam Deeds, quickly arrives on the scene. Unlike the dramatic tracking shot that unveils John Wayne as western hero Ringo Kid in John Ford's *Stagecoach* (1939), shot from below so that he towers above his Monument Valley backdrop, Sam is shown immersed in the landscape, crouching down to examine the scene.[3] Through this opening, Neil Campbell suggests that history is "the burier of secrets" and that Sayles is "excavating the geological layers of what is remembered, who remembers, how memories are constructed."[4]

The two men's exploration and discovery immediately anchors *Lone Star* to its distinct place and history. This location was one of the most challenging for the film crew to settle on, as it needed to have a specific kind of rolling terrain and flora. Missing the latter, the props department stepped in, and the crew found themselves planting cacti in the desert.[5] In the film's opening dialogue, as Cliff identifies local plant life, he proclaims, "You live in a place, you should learn about it." Meanwhile, Mikey uses a metal detector to search for bullets from which he builds sculptures. When Mikey calls out to share a discovery, Cliff jokingly responds, "Spanish treasure, right? Pieces of eight . . . from the Coronado expedition?" From the beginning, the location is tied to its colonial history.[6] When Sam later responds to the suggestion that they are on a crime scene, he further alludes to a contentious history, when he comments, "No telling yet if there's been a crime . . . but this country's seen a good number of disagreements over the years."

When Sam surmises that the skeleton on the rifle range was Charley Wade, he develops rapid suspicions that his father may his murderer. As he begins his investigation, Sam seems compelled to unveil darker truths about Buddy.[7] His approach to investigating his father's legacy is akin to conducting historical research. As Kimberly Sultze writes, his inquiry involves "looking at artifacts—the bones, badge, and ring—and making inferences; establishing chronology by examining historical records from the sheriff's office, the county, and the hospital, as well as his father's personal correspondence; and conducting interviews with the townspeople who lived in Frontera at the time."[8] While Buddy was revered in the community as the heroic force that overturned Wade and remembered for "presiding over a period of harmonious existence among the Hispanic, Anglo, African American and Native American

Figure 12. Sam visits Hollis's fishing boat.

people of Frontera," Sam remembers his father as more complex and complicated than his register in the public memory.[9] In pursuing his suspicions, though, others warn him to drop his inquiry.

When Sam visits Mayor Hollis Pogue at his fishing boat to discuss the body that was uncovered and suggests his father might be to blame, Hollis reminds him of the upcoming courthouse memorial dedication in Buddy's honor, pointing out that "It's a hell of a time to bring up old business." While Hollis says he understands Sam's motivations to target his father's legacy, he encourages Sam to leave the past alone: "Look at all this. Tackle, boat . . . All just to catch a little old fish . . . minding his own business down at the bottom of the lake. Hardly seems worth the effort, does it, Sam?"

Later, at the roadside trading post, Sam meets Wesley Birdsong (Gordon Tootoosis), who sells objects such as souvenir buffalo chips and a radio in the shape of the Alamo along an empty stretch of highway. Although a minor character, Birdsong had a close history with Buddy so that he is able to supply a telling piece of information—that Buddy was having an affair that "half the damn county" knew about.[10] However, he demurs from saying much more. In a similar manner to Hollis, Birdsong points to a rattlesnake skin: "Here. This big fella was sleeping in a crate at Cisco's junkyard. When I was going to open to see what was in her . . . [it] jumped right at my face. Scared me so bad I had to kill him without thinking. Be careful where you go poking. Who knows what you'll find." These overlapping warnings, which ultimately do not deter Sam, reinforce Sayles's idea "that you have to be careful of what you look for, because you might find it."[11] From the beginning, an inherent risk exists in dredging up "old business." But only through this recognition of the past does new understanding become possible.

When Sam confronts Hollis and Otis in the roadhouse late in the film with his conclusions about Buddy, Hollis sounds the often-told refrain about Buddy. "Your father had the finest sense of justice of any man I've ever known," he began, causing Sam to exasperatedly cut him off to add, "And my mother was a saint." Only when Sam explodes with the conclusions of his investigation—that Buddy had murdered Wade, embezzled money, and had an open affair—does Otis finally break from the established narrative to share what happened on the night of Wade's death.

In introducing the story, Otis begins with how Wade disrupted a poker game at the club that he had been cut out of; when he concludes it, Hollis is the one who is speaking. And so the scene itself implies

Figure 13. Buddy enters the roadhouse.

competing voices and competing points of view. Dual perspectives are also at work in the shooting of the flashback scene. Sayles explains, "When you see the close-up of the gun firing, the one which kills Charley Wade, there's one shot shooting left and there's another shooting right. Two people, different points of view. If you're one guy, it's an eyeline problem. Whose point of view is this from? So let's do it two ways."[12] In the flashback, Wade rages at Otis, his shouting silenced by music. As Wade turns to wink at Hollis, he pulls a gun on Otis's back, which recalls his execution of Eladio Cruz. A gunshot rings out. As the camera cuts to the door swinging open, Buddy yells out, "Charley Wade," at which point the camera shifts to reveal Hollis holding the gun. Buddy had arrived moments too late, just as Hollis shot Wade in the back.

Panning back to the present, Sam grapples with the realization that his father had not killed Wade. Explaining their decades of secrecy, Otis says, "Time went on, people liked the story we told better than anything the truth might have been." Hollis points out that if the discovery of Wade's body became public, Buddy would be a primary suspect. However, Sam decides against revealing the truth that Hollis was Wade's killer, reassuring Hollis that "Buddy was a goddamn legend, he can handle it." This decision marks a shift for Sam, who has relentlessly pursued the mystery of Wade's death throughout much of the film in the belief that his father killed Wade. At that moment, he realizes Buddy's legend is so powerful that it could negate any public speculation that his father was Wade's killer. Again, Sam's decision echoes the famous line from Ford's *Valance*, "When legend becomes fact, print the legend." In that film, the mistaken presumption that Ransom Stoddard is the killer of Valance, ridding Shinbone of a violent menace, has laid the groundwork for Stoddard's successful political career.

Throughout *Lone Star*, characters debate what memories should be honored, find evidence that prompts a revision of memory, and reject their own memories to follow new paths. After discussing Sayles's use of live transitions, continuous shots that move between time periods, I will look closely at several key scenes, including the courthouse dedication to Buddy Deeds, Delmore's discovery of his father's "shrine," and Sam and Pilar's final discussion at the empty drive-in. As Sam begins to question his father's involvement in Charlie Wade's death, new understandings of the past cause him to realize that his "story isn't over."

LIVE TRANSITIONS

In *Lone Star*, Sayles employed a distinctive cinematic technique for breaking down borders between the past and the present and visually representing narratives of memory. Using live transitions, in a single shot, Sayles directs the camera to pan seamlessly between different time periods with no breaks. This tactic departs from conventional film grammar. While other directors have used different strategies to depict flashbacks in the history of American film, most of those techniques involve dissolves or fades. These conventions were developed to mirror how the spectator would realistically intuit information. The fade-out/fade-in (whereby a scene fades in and out of darkness to convey the passage of time to mimic a rising/setting sun) is the typical approach in representing an elapse in story time.[13] But today, transitions between the past and present are often represented with a straight cut, joining two scenes without a transition, which creates a perceivable discontinuity for viewers.[14]

Sayles's live transitions, which he used seven times in the film, link "two *contiguous* spaces but two *disparate* time frames," creating what Janet Walker calls a "hybrid zone of memory."[15] This zone allows for different voices to merge as storytellers and thereby blend multiple perspectives of the past together. Sayles's tactic joins formal and thematic concerns, suggesting that history operates on a continuum so that the past continues to weigh on the present such that "these characters all carry their history around with them."[16] Visually, Sayles seems to take Patricia Nelson Limerick's suggestion to heart that the frontier would be better understood as la frontera, as a running story, in his manner of depiction.[17] He explains, "I wanted to reinforce the feeling that what's going on *now* is totally connected to the past. It's almost not like a memory—you don't hear the harp playing. It's *there*."[18]

Mercedes's restaurant early in the film marks the first time Sayles employs this technique. In a scene beginning in the kitchen, the camera follows Enrique carrying a steaming platter of food to Hollis, Fenton, and another unnamed "good old boy," as they fondly tell stories about Buddy over beers. The bright daylight streams onto the café's peach-toned walls and artificial flowers, as Sam awkwardly interrupts the men. Fenton asks Hollis to tell Sam the story of how Buddy ran Charley Wade out of town. When Hollis initially protests, "Everyone has heard that story a million times," Sam encourages him to continue, telling him he'd like to hear his version. Sam's request is an early indication that stories of the past have multiple "versions" that vary from teller to teller. As Janet Walker writes, "The truth about the past is represented as being multifaceted, subject to competing interests, and contingent upon the memory and will of the teller."[19]

As Hollis begins his description of Wade as an "old-fashioned bribe or bullets type of Sherriff," the camera follows Hollis's hand as he places down a basket of tortillas. After lingering on the tortillas for a moment, Wade's hand, identifiable by his Mason ring, pulls back a tortilla to reveal a ten-dollar bill. The camera then pans out to reveal Wade in the same café in 1957, only now it is night, and the tones muted greens. Many details, down to the platters of chicken-fried steak, remain the same, though in the past, the air is smokier due to cigars and cigarettes. Wade is explaining to Buddy his system for collecting bribes from then-owner Jimmy Herrera—"I scratch his back, he scratches mine." Buddy flatly refuses to accept bribes and demands that Wade leave town, which leads to a tense confrontation. Buddy never leaves his chair as Wade leans in, threatening to kill him. After Wade leaves the restaurant, Buddy calmly turns his head and requests, "Más cerveza, por favor."

The camera, panning right, follows Buddy's gaze and then falls on Sam back in daylight, in 1995, listening as Hollis repeats, "Más cerveza, por favor." Fenton admiringly reflects, "That Buddy was a cool breeze." Hollis describes the face-off as the catalyst for Wade's departure, as he supposedly left town that night, taking with himself $10,000 in county funds.

In addition to its use of the live transition, this scene establishes the central myth surrounding Wade's disappearance as well as Buddy's character. Cinematographer Stuart Dryburgh set up the confrontation between Wade and Buddy, via an off-kilter camera angle to Buddy's staying seated, that replicates a scene from Sergio Leone's epic 1968 spaghetti Western *Once Upon a Time in the West,* a film that also deals with the complexity of memory and familial succession.[20] This scene was also pivotal to Sayles's casting Matthew McConaughey as Buddy. Sayles reflects, "A key to the guy is that I felt he could have a confrontation with Kris Kristofferson, and it could be a stalemate. And he didn't have to stand up. It's not like he's going to hide. He's going to keep sitting there and doing it."[21] As crew member Caroline Hall Otis observed, McConaughey's early takes seemed to mirror Robert Duvall's Gus McCrae in *Lonesome Dove* (1989), but he quickly settled into his own rhythm.[22] Buddy's cool confidence in facing down Wade and his absolute refusal to take part in bribery and corruption set the stage for his rise as the town's uncompromising, yet fair, new sheriff. As Sam, who has spent his life living in the shadow of his father, launches his investigation into Wade's death, he repeatedly hears the same story: that Buddy was legendary and that his mother Muriel was "a saint," the implication being that he falls far short of his parents.

Hollis, who we later learn has a personal interest in shaping the narrative around Buddy, is the primary storyteller of this confrontation, both leading into and concluding the live transition. Other live

Figure 14. Buddy faces Charley Wade.

transitions in the film begin and end with different tellers, including Minnie Bledsoe, Otis Payne, Chucho Montoya, and Wesley Birdsong. This movement between tellers reinforces a sense of subjectivity regarding memory and how easily narrative changes as a function of teller. As Sam poses question after question to investigate Buddy's role in Charlie's death, he frequently receives answers that are incomplete or indirect.[23] From that, the burden of understanding the past falls to Sam and the film's viewers. Susan Felleman makes that point when she remarks that "often over-lapping fragments and versions of a tale [are] left for Sam and the audience to fit together."[24] Alan Barr also comments on this audience responsibility: "Just as Pilar recites to her students the dates of Texan history, with its national and ethnic wars, beginning in 1821, we, as audience, are confronted with the task of ferreting out the municipal and personal chronologies of Frontera and its principal citizens."[25]

The use of live transitions has broader implications for the way history transpires in the film. Tarancón Juan Francisco observes, "The past enters the present sequence of events as if past and present occupy the same space at the same time. In this way, the film undermines the linearity and homogeneity found in other more traditional representations of the West." *Lone Star,* then, "breaks the illusion of historical continuity and thus liberates the forces that are locked up in a linear explanation of the past.[26] Sulze makes a similar point:

> In *Lone Star,* Sayles does not hand us the history of the frontier in a handy package, dramatically posed, majestic landscapes, clear lines, better lit than real life and set to music. Instead, history is represented as a process in this film. It is embodied in the searches and transformations of different characters as they are investigating either the town's past or their parents' pasts. In that sense, *Lone Star* is a film about history, but also about the uses we give to history—and the impact we let it have on the present day.[27]

Again, Sayles's break with linear and contained frontier narratives models a vision of la frontera as a lens for understanding the past.

From a filming perspective, these transitions posed practical challenges for the crew. Dryburgh describes "mechanically, literally moving the camera" from one scene to another, noting, "It feels seamless because it is. There is no cut." However, Dryburgh recalls that in the early scene in the café, an aging Clifton James (Hollis) couldn't get out of the shot quickly enough, so the grips lifted him up in the chair to quickly replace him with McConaughey in the past.[28] When the crew transitioned the scene back to 1995, Hall Otis recollects the extreme focus on the set, "The dolly moves like butter, and the set dressers pull the 1957 façade down and splay on the floor—out of the shot—with remarkable facility.[29] It took fifteen takes to pull off the shot.

Ford's *Valance* also employs a flashback structure to reflect on the way memory, history, and legend are intertwined. Jim Kitses writes, "The structure underlines the role of memory: how does reverie relate to history? What is the effect of remembering? How do we construct the past?" Such questions are relevant to *Lone Star*, which should lead the viewer to consider how "we remember a giant of the past."[30]

THE BUDDY DEEDS MEMORIAL COURTHOUSE

The same early scene at Mercedes's restaurant where Sam encounters the "good old boys" also addresses the plan to dedicate the Buddy Deeds Memorial Courthouse, which stirs controversy. Hollis provides the film's only reference to Buddy's death, commenting to Sam: "Big day coming up. I wish we would have thought of it while he was still living. Went so unexpected." Fenton quickly adds, "Well, better late than never. Korean war hero, sheriff for nearly thirty years. The Buddy Deeds Memorial Courthouse." Sam comments, "You know, I heard there was a bit of a fuss," to which Hollis dismissively responds, "Nah, the usual troublemakers. Danny Padilla with *The Sentinel*, that crowd." The dialogue continues:

Fenton: Well, they call everything else in the country after Martin Luther King, we can't have one measly courthouse.

Hollis: King wasn't Mexican, Fenton.

Fenton: It's bad enough all the street names are in Spanish.

Sam: They were here first.

Fenton: Then let's call it after big chief shit in the bucket, that Tonkawa had the Mexes beat by a century.

Sam: Nineteen out of twenty people in this town are Mexican, Fenton.

Hollis: Well, there was a faction pulling for that boy who was killed in the Gulf War, Ruben . . .

Sam: Yeah, Santiago.

Hollis: Mexicans that remember know what Buddy was to their people. Hell, it was Mercedes over there that swung the deciding vote for him. She made it an even three-to-three and, as Mayor, I get to cast the tiebreaker. The old timers won't have any problem with it.

This exchange anticipates how Buddy's legend is both questioned and ultimately enforced in *Lone Star*. By pointing out Frontera's demographics and Mexican primacy, Sam acknowledges the competing stakes in cultural memory. The journalist Danny Padilla, who is Chicano and part of "that crowd," is seen as being a primary threat to enshrining Buddy's memory. Danny, who later confronts Sam with Buddy's questionable land dealings and vocally speaks out at a heated PTA meeting, advocates for telling the "full story" on Buddy Deeds and, by extension, a more complete historical perspective. Fenton, in contrast, feels threatened by the inclusion of non-white voices in historical memory, thus his desire to hold on to dominant Anglo-centered narratives. His backstory elaborates, "Fenton comes from a long line of Texas pioneers, people who *made* something out of this god-forsaken desert, goddammit, and that legacy should not be forgotten. If the Mexicans want their version of history let them cross over to the other side."[31] Danny and Fenton represent oppositional voices in the battle over cultural memory. Hollis uses Mercedes as an example that Mexicans will support enshrining Buddy, though we later learn that Mercedes's support for Buddy was much more personal.

As Sam makes his way to the memorial dedication, he is greeted by Jorge and Fenton, who comment "historic occasion, ain't it?" Sam responds, "Seems like we have another one every week." Fenton attributes the constant activity to Jorge's work with the Chamber of Commerce to "keep things humming." Their efforts to bring in tourists apparently include, as Sam mentions, "a ten-foot high catfish statue." This brief conversation suggests the way Frontera's leadership is attempting to define the town's identity for external consumption. Danny's backstory suggests that this is a point of frustration for the journalist whose efforts to provide historical perspective are checked by a town leadership that is "so intent on watching the dance between the dollar and the peso and figuring out how to profit from it, that his efforts fall mostly on deaf ears."[32] Sam's comment about the constant "historic occasions" is also in keeping with what Erika Doss refers to memorial mania, "an obsession with issues of memory and history and an urgent desire to express and claim those issues in visibly public contexts."[33] This obsession manifests itself in a proliferation of memorials, which like the debate surrounding the Buddy Deeds Memorial Courthouse, are subject to discussion over who and what should be remembered.

From Sam's conversation on Main Street, the scene quickly cuts to Cliff and Mikey, who come to realize that the bullet they found on the rifle range was the same sort that Buddy would have used—calling Buddy's legacy into question at the exact moment it was being solidified in stone. Back at the dedication, Hollis is speaking, describing Buddy as the ultimate "real Texan." When finished, Hollis somewhat reluctantly calls Sam forward, who keeps an even tone when addressing the crowd. He jokes, "I used to think there wasn't a place in this town you could hide from my old man. And now I'm sure of it." While Sam's comment is met with laughter, we later learn that Sam often felt monitored and controlled by Buddy.

Hollis then invites "my favorite council member and one of Frontera's most respected businesswomen Mrs. Mercedes Cruz" to cut the ribbon. Filmed from an unusual angle from above to capture Mercedes and the veiled memorial behind her, Mercedes turns toward the red ribbon to cut it. The shot shows a plaque at the base, reading "Buddy Deeds, 1930–1991, Beloved Sheriff and Community Leader. The Eyes of Texas are Upon You."

As Mercedes clips the ribbon, the blue veil drops to reveal the bronze memorial. Shown in relief on a flat vertical bronze slab, Buddy is depicted from just below the waist up, a sheriff's badge on his lapel, wearing a gun holster and cowboy hat. While he looks into the distance, his right hand is wrapped protectively around the shoulder a young Mexican boy whose face is turned into Buddy's torso. A voice in the crowd remarks, "It does kind of look like Buddy." Fenton adds jokingly, "You know, I think he's going to run that Mexican kid in for loitering." Polite applause punctuates the reveal.

After the ceremony, Sam briefly tries to intercept Mercedes, who turns and walks away from him without acknowledgement. Once she is in the distance, graciously greeting attendees, her expression becomes worried as her gaze lands on Sam and Pilar. They turn from the scene to take a walk along the Rio Grande River—the place where they used

Figure 15. Sam and Pilar walk by the river.

to privately meet as teenagers. As they walk, Sam admits to Pilar, "They cooked the whole thing up without asking me." Pilar responds, "People liked him," recalling a moment when he watched her at the school playground as if she were the only person there. She recalls a spike of fear that he might arrest her ("he had those eyes, you know"), but then brushes off her observation by adding, "It's weird what you remember."

As Sam and Pilar talk by the river, Sam provides more insight into his relationship with his father, telling Pilar that he "spent his first fifteen years trying to be just like Buddy, and the next fifteen trying to give him a heart attack." The backstory for young Sam describes the pressure he feels living in Buddy's shadow: "When Sam was little that was great and he was proud of his father, but now that he's reached his teens it is a heavy load to carry. Everyone knows him as 'Buddy's boy,' not as himself," making it "suffocating for a kid trying to stake out a little territory for himself."[34] While Sam thinks that he has found that freedom in Pilar, Buddy takes that from him as well. For young Pilar, she too has felt overlooked and undervalued in a strict household where she lives with the proud and inflexible Mercedes, who is haunted by the loss of Eladio. Her backstory reads, "Pilar is smart and good in school but feels lost sometimes, like her mother's character is so strong that Pilar might disappear, become just a part of Mercedes, another ghost in the house."[35] Pilar also realizes that once her mother discovers her relationship with Sam, it will be forbidden, which only intensifies her connection to him.

After present-day Pilar returns to class, a live transition returns Sam to their teenage years in the same riverbank location where they discuss whether to tell their parents about their relationship. When young Sam flashes with anger in saying his father doesn't need to know his business, Pilar points out that he will find out regardless. Sam's response, "What is he going to do, arrest us?" foreshadows a later scene between the teenagers at the Vaquero Drive-In. Embracing in a car, while the 1973 film *Black Mama, White Mama* plays on screen, Buddy's deputies aggressively disrupt the movie and pull the lovers apart as lights flash and car horns honk noisily.[36] The memorial dedication and reconnection with Pilar prompt Sam's personal memories of his father to surface. For the community, the memorial affirms Buddy's legendary status in the town, but for Sam, it further urges him to make the full story known. Two of the key agents in fighting for the memorial—Hollis Pogue and Mercedes Cruz—are later shown to have personal ties to Buddy that are closely veiled.

A revised version of the script dated April 4, 1995, contains an extremely brief scene not included in the final cut; in it, Hollis discovers that someone has spray-painted "Perdido!" over the memorial of Buddy. "Hooligans," Hollis responds as he examines the damage with two men from the Public Works Department. "It happens again we build a fence around it."[37] Earlier in the film, the journalist Danny has passionately shared the history of Perdido to Sam as they walk down Main Street, over Fenton's protests that the story is "ancient history." Danny explains that in 1963 the north branch of the river was dammed to make Lake Pescadero, which submerged an entire town nearby. In response to the protest that Perdido was a "squatters town," Danny exclaims, "People lived in Perdido for over one hundred years! Mexicans and Chicanos are deported, forcibly evicted by our local hero, Buddy Deeds, and his department. There was a bill from the state legislature. Families were split apart! A whole community was destroyed!" As a result, Danny continues, Buddy and Hollis ended up with lakefront property at "a fraction of market price." When Danny clarifies that he is not trying to come after Sam through his father and only wants the full story of Buddy to be told, Sam agrees. He says, "That makes two of us." For Sam, the self-interest and underhandedness of his father simply underscored the fallacy of Buddy's legend. Later, when Sam runs into Fenton and Jorge before the memorial dedication, Jorge reassures Sam that he has convinced a contact at *The Sentinel* to kill Danny's story, saying the contact agreed "it wasn't exactly news." Fenton quickly turns this "favor" on Sam, by using it to wheedle Sam's public support of the new jail, which Sam dismisses. Even though Danny's story of "Perdido" was quashed to curry favor with Sam and to win his political support, the early draft of the film suggests that suppressed histories will continue to spill over into the present.

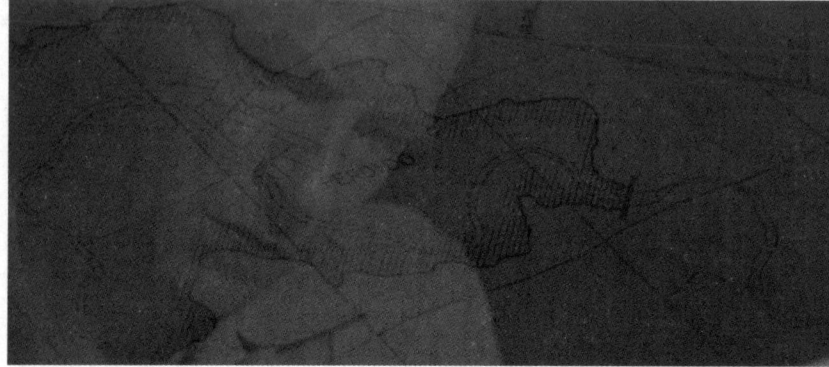

Figure 16. Sam examines a map of Perdido.

With the dedication of the Buddy Deeds Memorial Courthouse and the deleted scene of vandalism, Sayles anticipated contemporary debates about public remembrance and other notable examples of vandalism in the Southwest. Over the past decade, protesters across the US have targeted visible symbols of white supremacy and have called specifically for the removal of public statues of Confederate soldiers, slave owners, and conquistadors.[38] During the summer of 2020, when much of the nation endured a lockdown due to the COVID-19 pandemic, the May 25 death of George Floyd at the hands of a Minneapolis police officer sparked protests for racial justice across the nation and reignited debates over public statues. In the weeks that followed, dozens of statues and memorials to Confederate soldiers and generals, as well as other figures of historical oppression, were vandalized or removed. These figures of white power "that had been set in stone over long periods of time" had been subject to criticism for decades as "symbols of racism." Sturken writes, "The removal and destruction of so many monuments revealed a shift in public discussion about race, nation, and memory and a surging of memories of racial violence that had long been suppressed."[39] In the Southwest, monumental statues of Spanish colonizer Don Juan de Oñate proved to be a flashpoint for memorialization, with statues erected in Alcade, New Mexico, in 1993, in Albuquerque, New Mexico, in 2005 and El Paso, Texas, in 2006. In 1997, two anonymous activists sawed off the bronze right foot of Alcade's Oñate's statue, protesting the punishment Oñate had inflicted on men at Acoma Pueblo after an uprising. Responding to an outcry over memorializing and honoring Oñate, a convicted war criminal, as a statue, the El Paso statue of him was renamed "The Equestrian." In 2020, both the statues in Alcade and Albuquerque were removed from public view.[40] As implied with the memorial vandalism in *Lone Star*, attempts to honor what Kitses refers to as "giants of the past" grow complicated when deeply rooted memories emerge.

A SHRINE

In *Lone Star*, discovering material evidence is often key to uncovering new versions of the past. As Campbell notes, multiple characters are shown to be "collectors," from Otis Payne and his Black Seminole Museum, to Wesley Birdsong and his roadside trading post, to Bunny and her garage full of letters and photographs. They each "contribute to this 'piling-up' of alternative buried voices and versions of the past, providing a framework for Sayles' reconsideration of relations of memory and history."[41] Psychologist Mihaly Csikszentmihalyi has described how material objects structure the way we understand ourselves and our lives. Objects frame memories and provide evidence of events gone by, which justify that our identities and experiences matter. They help us maintain purposeful order, he writes, by revealing the owner's power, the continuity of self through time, and by giving evidence of one's place in a social network.[42]

Three generations of Payne men—Otis, Delmore, and Chet—reinforce Sayles's focus on the challenging relationships between fathers and sons and suggest how material evidence can shift long-held understandings of the past. As Delmore explains his family history to Celie, Otis left Delmore and his mother when he was a child to move in with a nearby lover and stopped communication. His mother later told Delmore that his father never asked about him. This abandonment shaped Delmore's upbringing and, presumably, his beliefs about personal responsibility, his commitment to duty and order, and his desire to live far from his painful childhood.

As described in chapter 1, Delmore is left unmoored because of his first interaction with Otis on his return to Frontera. Even though Otis expresses openness at getting to know Delmore's family, he, too, is guarded. While Delmore has lived most of his life without his father, Chet also suffers because of this loss. Chet views Delmore as inflexible and demanding and, like Sam, resists his father's constant "tightening screws." When Delmore becomes cognizant of how this familial strain affects Chet, he is prompted to pay a visit to his own father, showing up at Otis's home unannounced one evening. There Otis's wife, Caroline, greets him and urges him to come in to wait for Otis to return home.

In taking in the home, Delmore focuses on a framed newspaper article featuring Otis's award-winning hot sauce. He carefully ventures to Caroline, "You've been in this house for a while . . . ." After confirming that she has lived in it for eight years, she acknowledges that Otis has had a series of partners that neither she nor Delmore has met and then quickly offers to show him around. In an adjacent room, Delmore first notices more images of the Black Seminoles, which Caroline describes as "cowboys and Indian stuff." As Delmore's eyes scan the room, he visibly recoils when his eyes land on a wall of framed newspaper clippings celebrating Delmore's accomplishments. The most recent, "Payne Selected as Commander of Fort McKenzie," is dated March 2, 1995, and the earliest dates to his childhood: "Local Youth Wins State Science Fair." From the doorway, Caroline comments, "Kind of like a shrine, isn't it?" Collecting himself, Delmore questions how his father had acquired the clippings and learns that they came from his uncle. Ever since, the clippings have remained a source of real pride for Otis. Delmore, still coming to terms with what he is hearing, says, "My mother said he never asked about me." Caroline responds, "He never asked *her*." When Otis quickly ducks out of the house, Caroline calls after him, "Catch you later . . . Colonel." Played by acclaimed dancer Carmen de Lavallade, Caroline has a noticeably graceful bearing in her interaction with Delmore and is quietly amused in seeing how he draws his own conclusions about what she has shared.[43]

For Delmore, seeing his father's shrine to him pushes him into uncomfortable territory. Otis, who as a young man served in the Korean War and lived in Houston, had returned to Frontera to finance his next move, though having a young wife and child imposed restrictions and limits on what he could do.[44] After Delmore's parents divorced when he was seven, "the long-distance silence of his father and his mother's bitter comments built a family mythology that he has spent a lifetime reacting to."[45] With his recent discovery, Delmore suddenly realizes his father

Figure 17. Caroline observes Delmore.

was not as disengaged and uninterested as he has believed his whole life. Rather, in a similar way to his collection of materials for the Black Seminole museum, his "shrine" to Delmore was a way for him to channel his pride in his son's achievements.

The relatively brief visit to his father's home shifts a fundamental understanding Delmore had about his childhood and estrangement from his father. It also leads him to rethink the tight reins he has placed on Chet in hoping that he would attend West Point—a goal driven by Delmore's fear of Chet's facing the uncertainty of civilian life.[46] After visiting his father, Delmore connects with Chet in their kitchen where Chet is drawing at the table. While Chet makes a reference to the presumed plan of his joining the Army, Delmore expresses that "I wouldn't be disappointed if you chose to do something else with your life." Sensing an opening, Chet casually asks Delmore, covering his own interest, "Are we ever going to see your father?" Delmore immediately responds harshly, "My father . . ." before shifting gears and suggesting that they host a barbeque for Otis and Caroline the following weekend. Chet's excitement escapes him at this suggestion, which indicates that he already knows Otis "makes his own barbeque sauce." This scene promises that a different kind of relationship may form among the three generations of Paynes, as a way forward now exists because the misunderstandings and fears from the past that have haunted him have disappeared.

This shift in understanding as new information is shared, Anna Adams writes, reminds us "that historical interpretation is dependent on the nature of the sources."[47] Throughout *Lone Star*, the uncovering of the past leads to new possibilities for the future. Sulze writes, "Over the course of the film, Sam, Pilar, and Delmore all discover that they have gotten some things wrong about their parents' lives, and in the process, gotten some things wrong about themselves. These character transformations based on personal histories serve as metaphors for the re-examination of national history and identity."[48] Again, this reexamination aligns with Limerick's call that we reconsider Western histories as more comprehensive in how they highlight interconnections rather than distinctions. *Lone Star* calls for a more inclusive history that encompasses divergent group memories.

SAM AND PILAR

Sam and Pilar finally reconnect romantically when Sam waits for Pilar after work one evening. Pilar asks him to follow her to the diner, and the soundtrack for Sam's drive proclaims love as "a deep blue sea," and "an ocean road, longer than forever."[49] Moonlight streams through the windows of the café, as Sam and Pilar dance to Freddy Fender's "Desde Que

Figure 18. Bunny is paid a visit by Sam.

Conozco," a Spanish cover of Ivory Joe Hunter's "Since I Met You Baby." In filming this scene, Hall Otis notes, "the air is so redolent with love and loss and hope that my lungs can feel the pressure."[50] Spending their first night at Sam's apartment, Pilar notes the blankness of his walls, the absence of photographs, which Sam explains away when he tells her that the past is nothing he wants to look back on. Pilar questions, "Like your story is over?" When he admits he has felt that way, she responds, "It isn't. Not by a long shot."

Nearing forty, Pilar is a widow with two teenagers and reluctant to consider a new beginning. As she notes to her colleague, "I'm unmarried, not available." In Sam's case, he had an unfulfilling first marriage with an unbalanced football fan, has pursued careers—first for his father-in-law and then as sheriff—that do not suit him. And the constant question through is this: "Are you doing something that's about you or is this something that's about living up to the legacy that's been left to you?"[51] As a result, "Sam is the one who is going back into the past, he's the one who's digging the deepest."[52] Throughout *Lone Star*, it is Sam's insistence on unravelling the past that propels new possibilities for the future.

Well after Birdsong has told Sam about Buddy's affair, Sam pays a visit to his ex-wife Bunny and discovers with whom. Bunny's living room, filled as it is with Texas sports memorabilia, makes evident that she has dealt with the various losses of her own life by living vicariously through football. Sam's clean-slate apartment walls tell a different story of accommodation vis-à-vis the past. Material evidence of his family's history, we learn, has been left in a precarious position in Bunny's garage. He approaches the topic with Bunny, by asking "You haven't had one of your fires again?" After an extended and uncomfortable visit, Bunny snaps at Sam, "Your shit's still in the garage, if that's what you came for." As Sam combs through personal belongings, a close-up of his hands shows him uncovering a Zane Grey Western pulp magazine, a photograph of a toddler on a horse, records and certificates, and, finally, a letter in a scalloped envelope that begins, "Dearest Buddy."

The film's closing revelation that Buddy was having an affair with Mercedes, and Pilar was the product of this affair, suddenly places Sam in an incestuous relationship with his half-sister. This discovery strains the film's earlier discussion, voiced by Otis, that blood "only means what you let it." Sam shares this information with Pilar at the same drive-in where they had been driven apart as teens. In the film's present day, the drive-in has fallen into disrepair, with wildflowers pushing through the concrete and the screen missing large chunks. Sitting together on the trunk

Figure 19. Buddy and Mercedes.

of Sam's car, Sam presents Pilar with evidence uncovered in Bunny's garage—a photograph of his shirtless father, young and smiling, with his arms wrapped around a young Mercedes. The image substitutes for Sam's need to tell the full story; Pilar intuits that immediately.

Like Delmore's discovery of his father's shrine, this discovery overturns a long-held understanding of the past. Sam and Pilar had always believed their parents did not support them because of their youth or status as an interracial couple, only to find that they had been trying to prevent an incestuous relationship. This new understanding of their relationship offers them only two options—to end their romance, or to move on together knowing that their relationship is incestuous.[53] Despite the gravity of the taboo that they face, Sam and Pilar agree that they will disregard history and start anew. Their exchange goes as follows:

Pilar: So, that's it? You're not going to want to be with me anymore? I'm not having any more children. After Amado, I had some complications—I can't get pregnant again, if that is what the rule is about.

Sam: If I met you for the first time today, I'd still want to be with you.

Pilar: We'll start from scratch . . .

Sam: Yeah.

Pilar: Everything that went before, all that stuff, all that history—the hell with it, right? Forget the Alamo.

The film's closing line confirms Pilar and Sam's desire to "start from scratch." This decision, José Limón writes, is "based not on sexually transgressive ambivalence but rather on a clear recognition of their relative equality and the public continuation of their love."[54] Their choice to forget history (an especially notable declaration for a history teacher) and pursue their relationship, he argues, demonstrates a politics of negotiation that joins two social sectors and challenges stereotypic iconographies.[55] While Limón acknowledges this may be a utopian vision, Sayles has said, "It's clear to me, these are two people who should be together."[56] The film concludes with a wide shot of the empty drive-in with its damaged screen, as Patsy Montana's 1935 hit "I Want to Be a Cowboy's Sweetheart" leads into the credits.

The film's closing revelation of incest has drawn a range of critical reactions and scholarly interpretations. While *Lone Star*'s focus on patriarchal authority and incest have led some scholars to read the film through the lens of Freud's Oedipus complex, Mark Bould suggests that this approach can strip texts of their particularity, "so that they conform to the structure of myth, a unificatory tendency completely at odds with *Lone Star*'s politics."[57] In contrast, Kim Magowan argues that Sayles has

Figure 20. Sam and Pilar talk at the drive-in.

created a situation in which the extreme taboo of incest "does not have the usual tragic consequences." By combining incest with miscegenation, Sayles draws on racial politics in "partially legitimizing" incest.[58] Todd F. Davis and Kenneth Womack furthermore argue that Sayles "exploits the incest taboo as the vehicle for his analysis of the interconnected ethnic threads that constitute contemporary American life and the often uneasy relationships that continue to exist between the races"; and "for exploring the ways in which our shared history impinges upon the ethical choices that confront us in the present."[59]

For Sam and Pilar to confront this ethical dilemma, Sayles selects a communal meeting place, a site that reflects a need for connection and a collective experience. Rather than shooting in matching close-ups, he keeps them both in the frame for the full conversation. The drive-in is meaningful to Sam and Pilar as the place where they were pulled apart from each other as teens, but also, like the river, it provides a place outside of the community's gaze to meet and talk freely. Sayles reflects, "I wanted the sense that they are looking at the screen as if something may come up, but the screen is wasted. There are the ravages of the past."[60] The blankness of the screen is not without future possibility, that "something could be projected on that thing. But they're not the fourteen-year-old kids that they were. They've had some damage. Things have fallen away. They're different people. But that doesn't mean their love is dead." Sayles is clear that Sam and Pilar's decision to move forward together is one that makes sense for them individually but does not work on a societal level. For Sam and Pilar to have a future together, they must escape their personal histories and leave Frontera.[61] As Magowan observes, Sam and Pilar have always existed on the fringes of knowledge in Frontera as among the few who were not aware of their parents' affair. This makes their choice to stay together and start anew an easier one, as they "institutionalize an alienation that they have already been allotted."[62] However, their choice to start over is complicated by the fact that they will need to lie to Pilar's children about the nature of their relationship, which means that the lies of the past will extend to the next generation.[63]

Placing the final scene at the drive-in where Pilar speaks her line, "Forget the Alamo," before an empty screen suggests that it is not just history in the film, but also its manner of representation that must be rewritten.[64] Campbell suggests that the drive-in is a place where Pilar and Sam can "look up to the screen ready to 'project' their new vision upon it, ready to take over the role of the movie as the 'escape' from the everyday borders and restrictions of their lives and in their creative imaginings of alternative identities."[65] Significantly, while screens often serve as barriers, the drive-in's movie screen is shown with a sizeable hole in it that suggests through a visual metaphor "the film's ultimate contemplation of both the integrity and the permeability of borders."[66]

As this chapter demonstrates, *Lone Star* traces moments when characters discover that their perceptions of the past, both personal and collective, have been based on incorrect information. Although Sayles shows the truth as offering the potential for liberation, he demonstrates how its pursuit is fraught. Only through the direct confrontation of difficult histories, however, can new visions of the future emerge. That said, official, mythologized histories may shape the understandings of our communities and nation, but, in exploring what happens when certain narratives are forgotten, *Lone Star* suggests that long-silenced memories will ultimately rise to the surface.

3. | Institutional Change

Lone Star positions Frontera as a site of social and institutional change. As the town's demographics change, positions of authority are poised to turn over, particularly as white-dominated power structures face threat and are imperiled. The army base is in its final years of existence, a jail (or shopping center) may take its place, and new town leadership has begun to emerge. *Lone Star* offers the promise of new multicultural institutions and the acceptance of more voices. In her 1997 presidential address to the American Studies Association, Mary Helen Washington highlighted *Lone Star* as a "prophetic allegory of institutional change" that "projects a forward-thinking, but not utopian, vision of new multicultural social institutions."[1]

In producing this vision, Sayles responds to the culture wars of the 1990s, as liberal and conservative forces battled over historical representations. For instance, in 1991, art historian William H. Truettner curated the exhibition *The West as America: Reinterpreting Images of the Frontier, 1820–1920* at Smithsonian's National Museum of American Art to mount a critique of how mythologies of western heroism overshadowed the harsh realities of western settlement. In response to significant critical feedback, some of the exhibition's labels were rewritten in a more neutral fashion. The effort to depict a more inclusive West, where multiple stories compete to be heard, can spark anxieties about shifting demographics and the future of political institutions.

Steven Dubin observes that the redefinition of the Western genre easily predates the controversial exhibition. He points, for example, to revisionist films such as *The Wild Bunch* (Sam Peckinpah, 1969), *Little Big Man* (Arthur Penn, 1970), and *McCabe and Mrs. Miller* (Robert Altman, 1971), which reflected the resistance to authority during the Vietnam era. Decades later, these films were followed by *Unforgiven* (Clint Eastwood, 1992), which features a dime novel author W. W. Beauchamp (Saul Rubinek) leaving personal integrity behind to craft a mythic story of the West. Although *Unforgiven* deconstructed heroic Western myths to critical acclaim, *The West as America* faced backlash.[2]

The early 1990s also marked the quincentennial of Columbus's arrival in Americas, driving a wedge between American Indian activists and Italian-Americans who believed their heritage under attack.[3] In another nod to the reexamination of history, Congress passed a bill in 1991 that changed the name of the Custer Battlefield, commemorating the infamous 1876 battle, to the Little Bighorn Battlefield National Monument. The Persian Gulf War (early 1991) added another layer of context, as the brief military engagement and decisive victory stirred patriotic sentiments.[4] With museums, academia, popular culture, and politics their register, these events erected a complex stage for the sort of institutional change implicit in *The West as America* exhibition. *Lone Star* reflects similar cultural battles, as Frontera's educators, journalists, politicians, and community members of different backgrounds struggle to define a shared past, respond to changing demographics, and embrace new power structures.

The future of the town's institutions throughout the film remains in flux, evidenced by the proposed new jail and the closing army base. After considering Frontera's demographics and its history of white supremacy, this chapter will explore key scenes that explore the possibility of institutional change across law enforcement, education, and the military, including Sam's discussion about a future run for sheriff, a PTA meeting held in Pilar's classroom, and Delmore's conversation with Private Johnson. The backstories of Sayles's characters are particularly relevant in this chapter, as they lay out the histories and social conditions that motivate characters to advocate for, or against, institutional change.

FRONTERA'S DEMOGRAPHICS

The composition of Frontera is discussed in an early scene in Pilar's classroom, when Pilar explains to Chet's mother Celie that the school contains a "pretty lively mix," including "Mexican kids, Anglo kids, Black kids." The Black kids, she continues, are the smallest group, except for "a couple of Kickapoo kids." When Sam discusses the memorial plans with Fenton and Hollis, he points out that nineteen out of twenty residents are Mexican American. While the minority Anglo Americans have historically held positions of power in the town's leadership, Frontera appears poised for change, with the next mayoralty and sheriff seats projected to go to Mexican American candidates.

In Sayles's vision, Frontera has had a small Black population since the Civil War, which shrank during a job boom in California during World War II.[5] The small remaining community is amplified by the presence of Fort McKenzie but has not been a major participant in town governance. Wesley Birdsong, the roadside souvenir proprietor, is one of Frontera's few members of the Kickapoo nation. His backstory describes how the Kickapoo were historically pushed from the area that is now Wisconsin and Illinois and removed to a reservation in Kansas in the early 1800s. One band of the tribe branched off and settled near

Naciemento, Mexico, close to real-life Eagle Pass, where they lived in conflict with Texas settlers and were attacked by the US Army in the infamous McKenzie Raid, which occurred on Mexican land and mainly resulted in the deaths of women and children. Although part of the band moved on to Indian Territory, a small portion remained in Mexico, with many working part time in Eagle Pass. Birdsong chose to forge his own path, eventually befriending Buddy and similarly serving in Korea.[6]

Throughout *Lone Star*, many characters weigh in on the political and social changes that Frontera is facing. The film, accordingly, includes numerous references to whites losing power in Frontera, evidence of Washington's observation that white supremacy is "a system in decay."[7] Fenton, the bartender Cody, and the group of Anglo parents at the school PTA meeting "represent the perspectives of the white minority who feel their values, beliefs, versions of history, and political power under threat."[8] These community members want to see clear lines between "right and wrong, winners and losers, and 'us' and 'them' cleanly drawn."[9] In the scene leading up to Buddy's memorialization (discussed in chapter 2), Fenton expresses frustration at naming "everything else in the country after Martin Luther King" and that it's "bad enough all the street names are in Spanish." All the more vocal in articulating this worry is bartender Cody Wallace, whose bar features a prominent neon Lone Star sign in the shape of Texas and a handwritten notice that reads, "No Pesos."

According to Cody's backstory, he grew up in Frontera in the days when a white man "felt at home wherever he went—Darktown, Mexican section, out to Perdido even"—and the white minority ran the town in a way that Cody believes, "seemed right, seemed natural. They'd won the war, hadn't they?" As far as he is concerned, if Mexicans wanted to live

Figure 21. Sam visits Cody's bar.

north of the border, they would have to "learn to live by white people's rules." However, Cody has seen a shift in recent years and finds it hard to distinguish his hometown from Juarez. He was especially impressed by Buddy and felt that "When men like Buddy passed from the scene, that was all she wrote for Frontera, Texas. Adios."[10] Cody believes that Buddy was able to effectively serve as a "referee" in the "damn menudo" that characterized the border town.

When Sam pays Cody a visit at the bar, Cody tells him, "You're the last white sheriff this town's gonna see. Hollis retires next year, Jorge Guerrero's gonna take over. This is it, right here, Sam. This bar's the last stand. *Se habla* American, goddamn it!" In Cody's exchange with Sam, he reflects his belief that his bar is the last threshold of Anglo dominance, but "even in here, it's sliding away." Cody spots Cliff Hogan and Pricilla Worth, an interracial couple from the army base, holding hands at a booth in the rear of the bar. He uses them as an example to tell Sam, "We are in a time of crisis. The lines of demarcation are getting fuzzy. In order to run a civilization, you have to have clear lines of demarcation, between right and wrong, between this one and that one . . . . People don't want their salt and sugar in the same jar." As Kim Magowan points out, Cody's reference to mixing salt and sugar, rather than salt and pepper (which would be easier to distinguish) only adds to the fuzziness that Cody is calling to clarify.[11] As Sam responds, "If you mixed drinks as bad as you mix metaphors, you'd be out of a job." Cody's proclamation, "*Se habla* American," provides a similar mixed message. Magowan writes that "'American' and not English, is precisely what Cody must speak, particularly in this border town, where even rednecks need to have some proficiency in Spanish, and paradoxically defend their nativism with a cross lingual mixing."[12] Sam jokingly deflects Cody's assertions. At one point, Cody even claims that he's as liberal as the next guy, but Sam cuts in, "as long as the next guy is a redneck." For characters like Fenton and Cody, Melissa Clark-Jones writes, "The feeling of being threatened that emerges from shifting demographics, challenges "Anglos' numerical, political, and ideological dominance." This can feel like "an assault on, or a renovation of, historical truth at the community level."[13] In contrast, characters such as Sam, Pilar, and Otis demonstrate alternative, less oppositional possibilities for the future.

Sam's visit to Cody's bar also points to potential changes to the town's economy and physical landscape—and not just its leadership. As Sam joins Cliff and Pricilla in conversation, Pricilla mentions the uncertain future of the abandoned rifle range where Wade's skeleton was found. When she questions whether it was going to become the site of a shopping mall, Sam responds, "If certain people have their way, it's gonna be a new jail." Pricilla observes, "They're closing down military and putting up jails like 7-11 stores."

The town's political machinations to ensure the new jail surface when Sam runs into Jorge and Fenton on the way to the memorial unveiling. At the time, Fenton reinforces his desire for Sam to support the proposed new jail. Sam, though, protests that it is not needed, that Frontera is already "renting cells to the Feds for their overflow." Sam quickly deduces the men's true motivation: "It wouldn't be your construction company who'd get the bid on building this thing, is it, Fenton? And Jorge, you wouldn't be thinking about a couple dozen new jobs to dangle by the voters when you run for mayor next election?" Sam assures them that he will not campaign against their plans, but that if asked, he will give his real opinion. When they protest that they had backed him, Sam resists, pointing out that they just needed "someone with the name of Deeds" to push out his opponent.

According to his backstory, Jorge Guerrero admired Buddy but is less impressed with Sam. He also interprets Sam's ambivalence about his job as a sign that he does not appreciate those who helped him into the sheriff's office. Jorge, who is poised to run on the Democratic ticket to be Frontera's first Mexican American mayor after Hollis Pogue's retirement, is a life-long Frontera resident and experienced councilman. He has started to see a shift away from Anglo dominance, in part because "the huge ranching and real estate fortunes have already been made" and wealthy Anglos have left for other parts of Texas.[14] Jorge recognizes that the next mayor will be constrained by state funding from a "conservative, Anglo state government in Austin" and will be mostly monitoring everyday border commerce. An active member of the Chamber of Commerce, Jorge wants to attract wealthy Anglos from the north and Mexicans from the south to Frontera, "which means that the bloody, racist history of the region is best glossed over and made 'colorful,' rather than kept as festering resentment."[15] Instead, Jorge wants to remake Frontera as a site of investment and tourism. Jorge's vision recalls the scene in *High Noon* when the townspeople debate banding together against Frank Miller, seeming to agree that violence would set back the town's efforts to support schools and churches and scare off potential investors from "up north." Similarly, by projecting stability, Jorge believes that he is giving Frontera the best chance to progress. However, Sayles later suggests that such a commercialized vision of the future is limiting.

LAW ENFORCEMENT

Throughout *Lone Star*, Sam's disillusionment with serving as sheriff is obvious. He comments repeatedly that the job is not what he thought it would be, and he bristles at the commercial interests expressed by Jorge and Fenton. Sam's feeling toward his job seems to follow the fuzzy rationale he had for pursuing it in the first place. His backstory describes his motivations accordingly:

> Something vague about settling scores, something vaguer about maybe running across Pilar, widowed now with two children. The job has changed since Buddy's day and Sam finds himself in a position he has no training for, being administrator of a jail and a team of suspicious law enforcement personnel. He is smart and fair, though, and instead of resentment there is uncertainty in the ranks. What

> is this guy after? Much less ambitious than his sponsors hoped he would be, ironic, detached, Sam often seems to be watching himself play a part rather than wading into the politics of the Sheriff's office.[16]

Rather, it seems that Sam has fallen into the role of sheriff because he was not sure what else to do. When Pilar walks with Sam by the river, she asks why he returned to Frontera. He explains, "I got divorced, and I wouldn't work for my father-in-law anymore. And the fellas down here, they said they'd back me." Pilar observes, "You don't want to be sheriff." Sam responds, "I got to admit, it's not what I thought it'd be. Back when Buddy had it . . . Hell, I'm just a jailer. Run a 60-room hotel with bars on the windows." Community members also pick up on Sam's detachment. For instance, when he visits Minne Bledsoe during his investigation, she returns his introduction with "Sheriff Deeds is dead, you're just sheriff junior." In sizing up Sam relative to good old boys, Fenton claims, "You know that boy of his can't cut it. He's all hat and no cattle." As much as Sam tries to escape his father and what he stood for, his long shadow—"There will never be another like him"—proves hard to outdistance and leaves Sam a detached figure.

However legendary Buddy was in Frontera history, his decades as sheriff continued a long line of Anglo dominance in law enforcement. This lack of diversity is highlighted in the scene when Sam runs into Pilar for the first time in years at the police station. As she leaves, the camera slowly pulls away from Sam, looking forlorn, in front of a long row of portraits of past sheriffs, all white men. *Lone Star* focuses on the three most recent generations of sheriffs and, unavoidably, the transmission of white patriarchal authority.

Figure 22. Sam with photographs of previous sheriffs.

In Sayles's conception, Charley Wade is the descendent of the first Anglo settlers in Texas, who arrived at Santa Anna's invitation. He grew up immersed in a racially charged border mythology in which everyone was assigned a discrete "place" in society.[17] Wade lived through periods of lynchings in the 1920s and '30s, as well as deportations of Mexicans in cattle cars during the Great Depression; he came to understand these events as natural. This is evident in his threat to young Otis at the roadhouse when he tells him, "You learn to act your place, son. This isn't Houston." In Houston, Wade claims, "they let you boys run wild up there." Wade views it as his job to keep people—particularly Mexicans, Chicanos, and African Americans—in their "consigned place." When people stray, Magowan writes, "When, for instance, Eladio Cruz, Pilar's alleged father, transports immigrants across the border without Wade's sanction—Wade makes them pay."[18] Wade recognizes the importance of intimidation and uses his cruel intelligence and dry humor to aggressively hold on to power and his spot in the pecking order. Ben Wetzel, the Texas Ranger handling the forensics investigation of the Wade murder, recalls reacting to this intimidation as a child, when one wink from Wade caused him to pee his pants. Sayles adds, "What Charley Wade is best at, the most fun he has, is the existential poker of confrontation, the mean joke that dares to be answered, the invasion of other people's space, the pushing of buttons to make them squirm, all the while with his pistol and his reputation waiting in the hole."[19] For Wade, any potential threat or destabilizing force must be dealt with immediately. And as Fenton recalls, "Charley Wade were known to have put a good number of people in the ground." Although Wade perceived that Buddy had political skill, he instantly chafed at his rebellion.

After Wade's disappearance, as characters throughout *Lone Star* affirm, Buddy was emblematic of a period of harmony for Frontera's many cultural groups. In response to Sam's question about whether Buddy would accept bribes, Otis says, "I don't recall a prisoner ever died in your daddy's custody. I don't recall a man in this country—Black, White, Mexican—who'd hesitate for a minute to call on Buddy Deeds to solve a problem. More than that, I wouldn't care to say." Despite the community's reluctance to answer Sam's questions fully, his investigation into his father's past reveals that Buddy had indeed manipulated systems for his benefit. This included the eviction of the Hispanic community of Perdido (see chapter 2). In conversation with the janitor at his office, Sam learns that the janitor had once built a porch for Buddy during his the janitor's incarceration. Finally, Sam learns that once Wade had died, Buddy embezzled $10,000 from the county to further the appearance that Wade had intentionally left town. Buddy used it to set up Mercedes in her restaurant business, which he justified as a "widow's benefit" after Wade had killed Eladio. These illegal actions, if known, were quietly accepted by the community. In addressing Jimmy Herrara's illegal workers, which had prompted Wade's bribes, Hollis says Buddy "came to an accommodation." As Minnie Bledsoe recalls, Buddy would "look the other way" at their club designation, as long as they "threw votes in the right direction." Buddy offered an alternative to bribery and violence, but he still bent the law to support his own interests and did not unsettle existing power structures. Minnie's backstory demonstrates how she and others perceived the changing generations of sheriffs: "The Sheriffs who have come and gone over the years were like natural forces you had no control over—Sheriff Wade was a stretch of stormy weather, Sheriff Buddy a nice long season of relative calm and stability. That you existed at their mercy was just a given, something to deal with as best you could rather than something to question or fight against."[20]

After Buddy's death, the town's multicultural communities had no central or galvanizing leader, and so, motivated by the name Deeds, local businessmen banded together to support Sam's bid for sheriff. With this support, leaders expected Sam would operationalize their own vision of law and order and preserve the traditions of Frontera's sheriff's office. As Clark-Jones writes, "They would like him to authorize their social and economic dominance, to mitigate or stem the contemporary tide of change that demographic multiculturalism and democracy represent for them."[21] Other communities in Frontera, however, are ambivalent about Sam's inherited authority. Clark-Jones continues, as sheriff Sam has inherited power through patriarchal channels, on a personal level through his father, on a social level, and on a mythic level, "whose white-cowboy hat and sheriff badge he wears unaffectedly. . . . Like classic heroes, Sam's integrity will be in terms of public and private 'deeds.'"[22] Sam's isolated search to find the truth about Wade's murder, reflective of the film's iconic lone star, reveals the qualities that set him apart from his predecessors.

However removed Sam is from the violence that marked Wade's tenure, as noted above, he "seems adrift, unable to have replaced them with any more workable image of a masculine life."[23] Sam is uneasy as the recipient of this inherited authority. He refuses to engage "his father's style of corruption. He cannot lie and say the town needs a new jail just to satisfy the construction business and get himself re-elected."[24] To find himself, to write his own story, he needs to give up power and authority. Sam's conversation with his colleague Ray indicates that Frontera's law enforcement will be reshaped soon.

Ray's backstory describes him as a "good deputy—hard working, honest, sensitive when dealing with volatile situations," who is driven by a desire to serve his community, rather than politics. A people-pleaser, Ray understands that it is past time for Frontera to have a Mexican American sheriff and that he is the "most qualified candidate but doesn't want to rock the boat."[25] Although he sees Sam as honest and kind, he recognizes Sam's discomfort with authority and lack of interest in supervising the jail. None of that, however, would lessen his discomfort in running against Sam, despite the flattering community support he enjoys.

A passing moment early in the film shows Ray testing out his authority (as Sayles describes it: He's "practicing being the man") in bringing Shadow into the station after the roadhouse shooting.[26] Ray postures, "This ain't Houston, my friend. We're pretty much running things now. Our good day has come." Shadow snaps back, "You chumps ain't had a good day since the Alamo." In contrast to Wade's comments to young Otis, Ray implies Houston as a place that is still under an older order and as the site of progressive change. The uneasiness Ray evinces in confronting Shadow carries over to how he nervously approaches Sam outside the police station. After mentioning that he hasn't seen Sam at the jail much—following that with an awkward pause—he finally speaks what is on his mind:

Ray: I, uh, the committee, Jorge and Fenton and all, they uh, well they've asked me . . .

Sam: They want you to stand for Sheriff next election.

Ray: Yeah.

Sam: You'd do a good job.

Ray: Thanks. What about you?

Sam: I don't know if I'll still want it.

Ray: I just didn't want to go around your back, that's all.

Sam: I appreciate you telling me . . . . You think we need a new jail?

Ray: Well, Sam, it's a complicated issue.

Sam: Yeah right. You'd be a hell of a sheriff.

In this scene, Sam seems resigned to turning over the position of sheriff to someone more suited to the demands of the job and the political hedging that it requires. Although it is obvious Sam will be relieved to be unburdened of this inheritance, his future remains unclear.

Sayles views the generational change between sheriffs in *Lone Star* as symbolic of Texas history. In Wade, he sees someone who parallels a foot soldier at the Alamo, who finally benefits from having the upper hand and isn't going to relinquish it. In Buddy, he envisions a "live and let live,

Lyndon Johnson kind of guy," who is going to exercise authority, but in a more humane way.[27] For Frontera, Sayles considered Buddy a "useful legend" with "better intentions" than his predecessor.[28] Sam, in contrast, "is kind of the Hamlet of the piece. He belongs to that generation of people who don't know whether they really want to be the cop of the world, or even the cop of Frontera, Texas. They're uneasy with power and responsibility because they feel like, in the past, it's been abused so badly."[29] When Sam is not easily able to pin Buddy with the worst of his accusations, he is forced to step back and appreciate that his father was more complex than he believed. In stepping aside to pave the way for Ray, he imagines law enforcement will finally be run by a member of the town's majority, even though still beholden to Anglo business interests.

EDUCATION

As a history teacher, Pilar acknowledges that many groups have participated in Texas history, and her lessons include many stories about the past. Clark-Jones writes, Pilar "sustains a version of the past that is inclusive, democratic, drawn from both dominant and conquered groups' experiences and stories in constructing a newly legitimated, local and national history."[30] As *The West as America* exhibition indicates, attempts to tell more comprehensive stories about the past are often subject to backlash. In this case, Pilar's approach promises to threaten the transmission of cherished Texas mythologies, among them the Lone Star State and home of the famed Battle of the Alamo. These "mythic touchstones," embedded in frontier ideology, "have been part of the legitimation of heroism, conquest, and settlement of Texas and the United States for generations." Solidified through Western films, commemorative efforts, and place names, "they are at the heart of the

Figure 23. Disagreement at PTA meeting.

contestation and the content of textbooks and classroom pedagogy that shape a common cultural heritage."[31]

When parents indeed complain about Pilar's approach at an after-school PTA meeting, their protests occur because "those in power are protecting an unacknowledged canon, an institutional identity with a set of privileges which insures their cultural and/or political hegemony."[32] At the PTA meeting, Anglo parents push back over the kind of history that is being taught to "our children," only to have to be reminded by a Chicana parent that "they're our children, too."[33] The full argument unfolds as follows:

First Anglo woman: Just tearin' everything down. Tearin' down our heritage. Tearin' down the memory of people who fought and died for this land.

Chicano man: We fought and died for this land too. We fought the US Army, the Texas Rangers . . .

First Anglo man: And you lost, buddy. [Other voices: "Yeah."] Winners get the braggin' rights, that's just the way it goes.

Second Anglo man: People, people. I think it would be best if we don't view this thing in terms of winners and losers.

First Anglo woman: Well, the way she's teaching it, it's got everything switched around. I was on the textbook committee and her version is not . . .

Second Anglo man: We think of the textbook as a guide, not as an absolute.

First Anglo woman: It is not what we set as the standard. Now you people can believe whatever you want, but when it comes to teaching our children . . .

Chicana woman: They're our children, too, and as the majority in this community, we have the right . . .

First Anglo man: Well, the men that founded this state have the right to have their story told the way it happened, not the way somebody wanted it to happen . . .

Danny: Hey, hey, the men who founded this state broke from Mexico because they needed slavery to be legal to make a fortune in the cotton business.

Pilar: I think that's a bit of an oversimplification.

First Anglo man: Are you reporting this meeting, Danny, or are you runnin' it now?

Danny: Just adding a little historical perspective.

First Anglo woman: Oh yeah? Well, you call it history, I call it propaganda. Now I'm sure they got their own account of the Alamo on the other side, but we're not on the other side . . .

Pilar: There's no reason to be so threatened about this—[voices protesting]—Excuse me. I've only been trying to get across part of the complexity of our situation down here: cultures coming together in both negative and positive ways.

First Anglo woman: If you're talking about food and music and all, I have no problem with that, but when you start changing who did what to who . . .

Second Anglo woman: We're not changing anything, we're just trying to present a more complete picture.

First Anglo woman: And that's what's got to stop!

Second Anglo woman: Look, there's enough ignorance in the world without us encouraging it in the classroom.

First Anglo woman: Now who are you calling ignorant!?

The argument unfolds in Pilar's classroom, with the room's mise-en-scène reinforcing a range of Texas stories. Parents sit before a large map of Texas with a legend covering Mexico. On the blackboard is a picture of Native Americans dancing around a fire. Another wall is covered in historic maps, with an image of a cowboy at the head of a wagon train. No images of black people appear on any of the walls, however, nor are the images of Native Americans that do appear seemingly identified in their native lands.[34] The group itself is made up of Anglos and Mexican Americans parents and teachers, while the smaller groups of African American and Kickapoo parents have no representation at all. In addition, the group's varying body language suggests how open or closed they are to accepting more complex historical narratives. As Washington notes, "Those who refuse to cross ideological borders sit with arms locked across their bodies and their bodies locked rigidly in their chairs.[35] While the first Anglo woman suggests that it is acceptable to recognize the "food and music" of other cultures, overturning established institutions is not. As was true of *The West as America*, revisions to a cherished frontier myth are seen as threatening.

Alan Barr writes that while Pilar is teaching a "legitimate, balanced version of Texas history," the argument at the meeting "illustrates the emotions beclouding any clear, objective reading of the past."[36] Though Pilar defends her approach to try to "get across the complexity of our situation, with cultures coming together," she is unable to break through these emotional ties to beloved myths. The school principal attempts to serve as the group's moderator by trying to appease the angry parents. He frames the school's textbook as a guide, which presumably could be supplemented. Mark Bould observes, "Thus, while appearing to speak from a position without its own specific content and which seems to rise above such petty disputes, he nonetheless tacitly supports one view of history of being predominantly correct and only in need of tinkering or rounding out."[37] Ultimately he fails to bring any resolution to the conflict.

Washington appreciates Sayles's decision to leave this exchange unresolved, "allowing," as she puts it, "messiness as an inevitable part of the cultural menudo." She continues, "What I love about Sayles's depiction of this process is that he doesn't allow differences of language, politics, historical vision, etc., to dissolve in a soothing movement toward consensus; he presents the multicultural moment as one of tension, struggle, discomfort and disagreement."[38] While these struggles are challenging for those involved, "they affirm tolerance and democracy both ideologically and dramatically, through their content and form."[39]

This scene is especially reflective of the culture wars of the 1980s and 90s "in which issues of identity politics, multiculturalism and the representation of U.S. history came to the fore, often embedded in the looser exchanges and controversies over so-called political correctness."[40] Campbell writes that "figures such as Lynne Cheney, E. D. Hirsch, Allan Bloom began to attack newer teaching methods for addressing American history."[41] Cheney, particularly, argued in 1998 that "history textbooks needed to be like those of the 'early decades of the century . . . filled with stories—the magic of myths, fables, and tales of heroes,' providing 'symbols to share . . . helping us all, no matter how diverse our backgrounds, feel part of a common undertaking.'"[42] Sayles has pointed to a conservative husband and wife team of the Texas-based Educational Research Analysists, Mel and Norma Gable, who judge the merits of texts based on their Christian messaging and support of Reaganomics.[43] Because of the size of the textbook market in Texas, the group had the power to influence texts across the country, privileging ideological versions of the past. The sentiments expressed by Cheney and the Educational Research Analysis rejected scholarly and popular culture movements to embrace multicultural representations as more reflective of lived reality.

As Domino Renee Perez describes in the essay "Past is Present," which accompanies the Criterion Collection's 2024 release, the scene at the school seems to look forward: "capturing the state's ongoing attempt to advance a single version of Texas history through the 1836 Project." Passed in 2021, the 1836 Project (named for the year that Texas declared independence from Mexico) is a state law that requires a "patriotic" telling of Texas history. After a year of effort, a nine-member committee headed up the production of a fifteen-page pamphlet highlighting the state's economic prosperity and business opportunities, which, as happens, now becomes the possession of all new drivers in Texas when they receive their license. The motivation for this pamphlet, Governor Greg Abbott explained at the bill signing, was to "never forget why Texas became so exceptional in the first place."[44] Historians reviewing the pamphlet noted that its celebratory focus omitted many other realities. This includes, Perez notes, "severely minimizing the roles of Mexican, American Indian, and Black populations in the state's history. In other words, what was true in Frontera, Texas, in 1996 is now true for the whole state. Then again, perhaps it always has been."

While Texas has continued to grapple with how to frame state history, and debates over textbooks have become common nationwide, the Western genre has located the schoolroom as a generative site for producing US citizens. In films such as Ford's *Searchers* and Zinneman's *Shane*, early homesteaders are framed as a part of first stage of settlement that will eventually lead to new institutions, including schools and churches. In Ford's *My Darling Clementine* (1946), the presence of a schoolteacher promises to serve as a civilizing force. But even as the Western genre is frequently associated with the wide expanses of Monument Valley and other grand landscapes, the role of institutions is also significant in representing national progress. Interior scenes—at times compressed, noisy, and complicated—are often more compelling in depicting struggles over defining nationhood. For instance, in Ford's *Stagecoach*, it is the tight proximity of passengers of varying social backgrounds forced together in the stagecoach as they battle the external threat of the Apaches that unifies the group.[45]

In Ford's *Valance,* interior spaces, whether the newsroom, the kitchen, or the schoolroom, are central to group formation. In an extended scene, the schoolroom is highlighted as a place where national identity is forged. Jim Kitses writes, "The frontier school constructed by Ford for Hallie and her classmates is a multicultural mix of reluctant cowboys, proud Swedish immigrants, the eager offspring of Andy Devine's prodigious Link Appleyard, the black Pompey and Hallie herself. Ford celebrates the grassroots pioneers learning to read, the humble immigrants, the ex-slave, the cowboys and dog-faced ex-soldiers."[46] As lawyer Ransom Stoddard stands before a chalkboard, he proclaims that "Education is the basis of law and order" in neat cursive. Surrounding that board is an image of Abraham Lincoln and an American flag, as Stoddard stresses the importance of the free press and of every vote counting, before urging Pompey to recite the Declaration of Independence. The multicultural and diverse classroom serves as a microcosm of the emerging nation.

Although the schoolroom scene in *Valance* does reflect an early vision of multiculturalism, it also operates to reinforce what John Bodnar calls an "official culture" that mediates a variety of localized interests to promote "a nationalistic, patriotic culture of the whole."[47] In *Lone Star,* again, competing interests fail in achieving a neat resolution. As Campbell determines, "The notion that history is fixed and final, 'out there' and official, written down in textbooks and taught from one generation to the next, is questioned through the intersecting and contradictory memories of Frontera's multicultural citizens whose different 'versions' structure the complex layering of the film."[48]

MILITARY

While Mexicans and Anglos tangled for primacy in running Frontera's law enforcement, education, and governance, Sayles questions where the Black community fits in. As Pilar points out, Black kids were the "smallest group" at school, and, at one point, Otis remarks, "There aren't enough of us to run anything." In Otis's initial conversation with Delmore, he identifies Holiness Church and Big O's as the only places where Black people feel welcome in Frontera. Locating the army base Fort McKenzie in Frontera provides Sayles the opportunity to introduce more African American characters and thus to create a fuller "microcosm of race in the United States."[49] Sayles envisions the Black community in Frontera as "an enclave, one small neighborhood in an army base, which is this artificial little world, and you really knew when you were in that section of town."[50] The base is a staple Frontera's economy and a major employer of its Black community.[51] However, this group exists in flux, "for those who live on the base are not rooted in Frontera's past in the same way as the locals."[52] With Fort McKenzie on the precipice of closure, and Delmore saddled the role of lame-duck commander, the future for this community is uncertain. As Sam acknowledges to Wetzel, closing Fort McKenzie will "pull a lot of jobs out of this county."

In first imaging Fort McKenzie, Sayles was influenced by the racial politics of the recent Persian Gulf War. During this war, he has said, Black soldiers operated as mercenaries of a sort because, as they confessed, "this was the best job I could get."[53] The army seemed to be a place where "a certain degree of equal opportunity" looked to exist, where one could advance in society if one were willing to operate as a hired gun, even if the outcome worked against larger group interests.[54] Along the way, Sayles also drew on his knowledge of Buffalo Soldiers and Negro-Indian scouts, who helped whites battle Native Americans—precisely those bits that help to inspire Otis's Seminole museum. Rachel Adams writes that in *Lone Star*, "The haunting presence of the Black Seminoles recalls the historical injustice of slavery that stains the American past, as well as the ways the histories of blacks and Native Americans have been conjoined in the U.S. Southwest."[55] For the Paynes, ongoing ties to the military not only provide a means of belonging but also reflect broader historical and social inequalities.

These constraints are further amplified in Private Athena Johnson's conversation with Delmore in the wake of a failed drug test. Athena first appears in the film during the shooting a Big O's club, when an ex-boyfriend, Shadow, has trailed her to Frontera and shot her dance partner out of jealousy. In a following interrogation with Mike and Pricilla, Mike expresses empathy, noting that Athena has "pulled herself up out of bad situation," though Pricilla will have none of that, "Well, she's going to slide back into it." When Athena is called in to face Delmore, when his initial questioning falls flat, he tries to understand her motivations for joining the army. Athena reveals that she is not motivated by patriotic outcomes or national strategy. But rather than try to find her place in a chaotic outside world, she has chosen to join the army, which has given her security, if not goals and a sense of the future. And so the army for her is a world apart from her unstable homelife, which forced her to survive a day at a time.[56]

She explains, "It's their country. This is one of the best deals they offer." When Delmore asks why she thinks they are let in on the deal, she responds, "They've got people to fight. You know, Arabs, yellow people whatever. Might as well use us." Delmore, who moves from rigidness to empathy over this speech, encourages her to think about her fellow soldiers as a starting point for engagement. He tells her,

Figure 24. Delmore and Athena talk.

> It works like this, Private. Every soldier in war doesn't have to believe in what he's fighting for. Most of them fight just to back up the other soldiers in their squad. You try not to get them killed, you try not to get them extra duty, you try not to embarrass yourself in front of them. Why don't you start with that?

Athena, visibly surprised, responds, "Yes, sir," salutes and adds, "Thank you, sir," as she is dismissed.

Delmore's backstory suggests that he, too, struggles with the question of what his involvement in the army has really meant:

> Peacetime is hard on a warrior. Too much time to think. You've seen men you knew and cared about killed horribly—for what? You've chiseled yourself into an efficient weapon—for who? You're a black

> man serving a government with policies both foreign and domestic that are covertly and overtly hostile to black men—why?[57]

His conversation with Athena forces him to face the questions that he has worked hard to suppress, "moving from a kind of desperate certainty toward the hazy and frightening world of mixed motives and conscious alienation."[58] After his abandonment by Otis at a young age, Delmore has since craved the order and predictability of military life, particularly during the social upheavals of the 1960s, and sought to minimize any sense of ambiguity. This questioning, along with his new understanding of his father (see chapter 2), helps to break down some of the uncompromising stances that he has held on to as protection so that he can face larger, more challenging questions about his family and nation. In *Lone Star,* though the military presents opportunities for members of a marginalized community to find security and connection, its rigid structure can obscure complex social realities.

ENACTING CHANGE

Even as characters such as Cody argue for maintaining "lines of demarcation," *Lone Star,* as Campbell observes, "ultimately questions the rigidity of these borders and frontiers by demonstrating that their apparent authority can be challenged by individual choices and collective, communal change."[59] While opportunities exist to cross borders and challenge authority, *Lone Star* also acknowledges the weight of the past that carries through generations. In Sam's conversation with Bunny, his ex-wife imagines this weight in a literal way—the weights pressing down on her beloved football players who stand in for the crushing pressure of her father. The heaviness of the past "may or may not be overcome to allow change to take place."[60] Before we can imagine new possibilities for the future, Sayles notes that we must contend with this historical weight, "It's something we carry with us and it can be useful or it could be destructive." When destructive, "the only way to counter that is to be really honest about what happened."[61] Campbell adds, "In Sayles' new history, knowing about the past is vital as a way forward rather than as something to dwell upon or be imprisoned by, existing as part of a multifaceted spatial appreciation of living in the West with its many stories and many peoples."[62]

These efforts to face history to enact change must occur on both an individual and an institutional level. As Washington writes, "*Lone Star* insists that personal cross-cultural experiences only become comprehensible and liberatory when they are connected to a relevant institutional history."[63] We see that in Amy Lonetree's discussion of contemporary tribal museums and the need they satisfy for truth-telling within an institutional context. She also urges an additional need for a decolonizing museum practice that addresses legacies of "historical unresolved grief."[64] Only "by speaking the hard truths of colonialism" can spaces of healing and understanding develop. Similarly, through the medium of film, Sayles suggests that the only way to move forward from the past to allow for institutional change is to directly confront what has occurred. With this understanding, visions such as Jorge's, of a glossed over, sanitized version of history, has little chance of moving Frontera forward. The better alternative is Pilar's classroom model, which embraces multiple and conflicting histories without insistence on resolution. Only then is it possible for new multicultural institutions to emerge.

4. | The Ongoing Borderlands

During Ronald Reagan's second inaugural address in 1985, he evoked the defeat at the Alamo and paid tribute to westward expansion as core elements of national character:

> the men of the Alamo call out encouragement to each other; a settler pushes west and sings his song, and the song echoes out forever and fills the unknowing air. It is the American sound: It is hopeful, bighearted, idealistic—daring, decent and fair. That's our heritage, that's our song. We sing it still. For all our problems, we are together as of old.[1]

Patricia Nelson Limerick reflects that, in the wake of decades marked by a troubled engagement in Vietnam, rising American Indian activism, and the environmental costs of conquest, national frontier ideologies would presumably have become more complicated.[2] However, she also acknowledges that historical thought and popular culture move at varying paces, and the resonance of the frontier has continued to persist.

Over the course of this text, I have considered how *Lone Star* envisions American nationhood—its boundaries, the relationship between official history and memory, and its institutions and production of citizens. The themes underlying *Lone Star* have proved prescient of today's ongoing cultural and political struggles—including border control, memorialization, and how history is taught. In chapter 2, I have outlined examples of recent Western films that follow Sayles in taking up Limerick's vision of la frontera. As an art historian, I wish to close this

Figure 25. The Alamo.

project by highlighting other visual artists that draw on similar themes, providing new approaches to examining history, memory, and the contemporary border.

On February 23, 2018, to coincide with the date of the famous siege of the Alamo, *The Other Side of the Alamo: Art Against the Myth,* a three-part exhibition, opened at San Antonio's Galería Guadalupe. The exhibition, curated by Ruben C. Cordova, includes twenty-six San Antonio-based Chicanx artists engaged in reexamining the myths surrounding the Alamo. Cordova explains, "The Alamo is commonly touted as the 'Cradle of Texas Liberty,' but that appellation overlooks the fact that its legacy has been to subvert the liberty of people of color."[3] The exhibition's featured artists addressed this subversion, highlighting suppressed narratives through paintings, film, flags, photographs, sculptures, and installations. The exhibition was inspired when Cordova began researching Con Safo, a Chicano art collective founded by Felipe Reyes in South Texas in the late 1960s to increase Mexican American cultural representation. Reyes's work anchors the exhibition, which starts with his painting *Sacred Conflict* and depicts the Alamo with the United Farm Workers flag raised in the foreground. Other works were included from Con Sabo's early activist period, and still others were commissioned for the exhibition.[4]

In Albert Alvarez's *How the West Was Won* (2018), an acrylic on paper collage, he incorporates popular culture images related to the Alamo over a broad swath of history. Figures include Ozzy Ozbourne, who drew attention for urinating on the Alamo in 1982; Phil Collins, who owns the world's largest private collection of Alamo artifacts; the legendary Davy Crockett; and an American soldier killed in the historic battle. Connecting the images are phrases like "White Greed" and "Ethnic Conflict."[5] The exhibition's final gallery considers the legacies of the Alamo myth, the US conquest of Mexico, and includes Con Sabo member Jose Esquivel whose *Dreamers in Space* was part of the installation. This work addresses contemporary immigration concerns, with Deferred Action for Childhood Arrivals (DACA) recipients wearing graduation regalia floating in a cloud-filled night sky, itself an update of René Magritte's surrealistic *Golconda* (1953).[6] Esquivel explains, "The political reality for the Dreamers is not knowing where they belong, so they are suspended in space."[7] The painting depicts the Dreamer's arms extended, martyrs to broader political forces.

Other contemporary artists addressed experiences of border crossing. Luis Valderas, whose graphite and Prisma-color *A Line Beyond the Sand* (2007) was included (he had produced the site-specific installation *Black Dream Place* at the same gallery in 2013). Drawing on media such as latex, Styrofoam, aluminum tape, and mirrors, the installation placed an ancient hero's journey in a modern world by focusing on the mysterious, unnerving, and transformative aspects of border crossing. A video animation "*TrainRiverTracks*" was projected into the space and engaged the viewer into carefully stepping through a virtual border—an experience that is meant to "confront a multitude of fronteras" to "unsettle and rattle memories of stepping across all kinds of borders—an experience that transcends."[8]

In 2015, the interdisciplinary Indigenous arts collective, Postcommodity, made up of Cristóbal Martínez and Kade L. Twist, and prior collaborators Raven Chacon and Nathan Young, installed their highly visible art installation *The Repellent Fence* at the border near Douglas, Arizona, and Agua Prieta, Mexico. The largest binational land installation to be installed on the US/Mexico border, the temporary work tethered twenty-six "scare-eye" balloons, each ten feet in diameter, floating a hundred feet in the air across a two-mile stretch of border. According to the collective, the balloons replicate an "ineffective bird repellent product" that coincidentally featured "indigenous medicine colors and iconography" used by Indigenous peoples across the Americas for thousands of years.[9] Their work was intended to "bi-directionally reach across the U.S./Mexico border as a suture that stitches the peoples of the Americas together—symbolically demonstrating the interconnectedness of the Western Hemisphere by recognizing the land, indigenous peoples, history, relationships, movement and communication."[10] In

2017, the project was featured in a documentary about its construction, *Across the Repellent Fence.*

Since 2008, as part of his long-term project *La Frontera: Artists Along the US/Mexican Border,* New York–based photographer Stephen Falke has been photographing artists of all types—visual artists, writers, dancer, designers, and musicians—over the length of both sides of the border. This project resonates with Falke because of his upbringing in Germany when it was still divided by the Berlin Wall between East and West; he sees the growing steel wall between US and Mexico similarly, particular in its fostering both psychological and geographic divides. His project's intent is to "shine a spotlight on the vibrant cultural activities and cross-border opportunities that exist despite the tremendous challenges in this bi-national region."[11] With work featured in nearly twenty exhibitions in US and Mexico, Falke's more recent work spotlights migrants and migration, including the opera trio Artistas Fronterizas, who perform on both sides of the border; and artist Alvaro Enciso, who honors migrants who did not survive the border crossing by placing crosses in the Sonoran desert. Architects have also developed projects that encourage engagement rather than division, such Ronald Rael and Virginia San Fratello's award-winning *Teeter-Totter Wall,* which places the junction point of a series of pink seesaws at the steel border wall and allows for children on both sides of the wall to play together.[12]

Through a range of media and forms, these visual artists seek to bring, as Sayles had done with *Lone Star,* difficult histories to the surface, blur established borders, and find new points of connection across cultures. As characters in *Lone Star* express their desire to "start from scratch" by confronting historical struggles and telling more complex stories about the past, it becomes possible to envision a new future.

NOTES

INTRODUCTION

1. Richard R. Flores, *Remembering the Alamo: Memory, Modernity, and the Master Symbol* (University of Texas Press, 2002), xiv.

2. Flores, *Remembering the Alamo*, xvi.

3. Juan A. Tarancón de Francisco, "Film Genre and the Power of Symbolic Thought: The Challenge to the National History Paradigm in John Sayles' *Lone Star*," *Quarterly Review of Film and Video* 29 no. 5 (2012): 410.

4. Gloria Anzaldúa, *Borderlands/La Frontera: The New Mestiza: The Critical Edition*, Ricardo F. Vivancos-Pérez and Norma Cantú, eds. (Aunt Lute Books, 2021), 61.

5. Interview, John Sayles by Gregory Nava, Lone Star Criterion Collection, 2024.

6. Interview, Sayles by Nava.

7. Jim Kitses, *Horizons West: Directing the Western from John Ford to Clint Eastwood* (British Film Institute, 2004), 29.

8. Matt Zoller Seitz, "Director John Sayles on the Making of *Lone Star*," *Texas Highways*, January 18, 2024, accessed March 15, 2024, https://texashighways.com/culture/director-john-sayles-on-the-making-of-lone-star/.

9. Gavin Smith, ed., *Sayles on Sayles* (Faber and Faber, 1998), 217.

10. Seitz, "Director John Sayles."

11. Alan P. Barr, "The Borders of Time, Place, and People in John Sayles's *Lone Star*," *Journal of American Studies*, Vol. 37, no. 3 (2003): 373.

12. Kimberly Sultze, "Rewriting the West as Multi-Cultural: Legend Meets Complex Histories in la Frontera in John Sayles' *Lone Star*," *Film & History* 33 no. 2 (2003): 20.

13. John Sayles, "Borders and Boundaries: An Interview with John Sayles," interview by Dennis West and Joan M. West, *Cineaste* 22, no. 3 (1996): 14.

14. Thomas Schatz, *Hollywood Genres: Formulas, Filmmaking, and the Studio System* (Random House, 1981), 63.

15. Lee Clark Mitchell, *Late Westerns: The Persistence of a Genre* (University of Nebraska Press, 2018), 5.

16. Sultze, "Rewriting the West," 24.

17. John Sayles, *Thinking in Pictures: The Making of the Movie Matewan* (De Capo Press, 1987), 17.

18. Tarancón de Francisco, "Film Genre," 412.

19. Tarancón de Francisco, "Film Genre," 410.

20. Mary Helen Washington, "'Disturbing the Peace: What Happens to American Studies If You Put African American Studies at the Center?': Presidential Address to the American Studies Association," *American Quarterly* 50, no. 1 (1998): 13.

21. Washington, "Disturbing the Peace," 14.

22. Janice Radway, "What's in a Name? Presidential Address to the American Studies Association," *American Quarterly* 51, no. 1 (1999): 3.

23. Neil Campbell, "'Forget the Alamo': History, Legend, and Memory in John Sayles' *Lone Star*," in *Memory and Popular Film*, ed. Paul Grainge (Manchester University Press, 2003), 167.

24. Campbell, "Forget the Alamo," 167.

25. Megan Ratner, "Megan Ratner Discusses *Lone Star* with Director John Sayles," *Magazine of Independent Film* 4, no. 4 (1996).

26. Sultze, "Rewriting the West," 20.

27. Helen Barlow, "Crossing the Borders," *New Zealand Herald*, March 6, 1997.

28. Melissa Clark-Jones, "*Lone Star*: Renovation of the American Dream," *Studies in Popular Culture* 20, no. 3 (1998): 62.

29. Sultze, "Rewriting the West," 24.

30. Smith, ed., *Sayles on Sayles*, ix–xii.

31. Interview, Sayles by Nava.

32. Hugh Linehan, "Finding the New Frontier: Independent Film-Maker John Sayles Talks to Hugh Linehan," *Irish Times*, October 4, 1996.

33. Linehan, "Finding the New Frontier."

34. Scott Tobias, "Interview: John Sayles on *Lone Star*," *The Reveal*, January 10, 2024, accessed March 15, 2024, https://thereveal.substack.com/p/interview-john-sayles-on-lone-star.

35. Interview, Sayles by Nava.

36. Michael Doherty, "The Movie Guide Interview: Sayles Oriented," *RTE Guide*, October 14, 1996.

37. Sayles, *Thinking in Pictures*, 45.

38. Matt Schimkowitz, "John Sayles on *Lone Star*, the State of TV, and Making Movies on the Border," *The A.V. Club*, January 16, 2024, accessed July 20, 2024, https://www.avclub.com/john-sayles-lone-star-criterion-collection-interview-1851166384.

39. Bill Friskics-Warren, "Kris Kristofferson, Country Singer, Songwriter and Actor, Dies at 88," *New York Times*, September 29, 2024, accessed January 19, 2025, https://www.nytimes.com/2024/09/29/obituaries/kris-kristofferson-dead.html.

40. Wilson Chapman and Harrison Richlin, "Kris Kristofferson's Best Roles: 'A Star Is Born,' 'Heaven's Gate,' and More," *IndieWire*, September 30, 2024, accessed January 19, 2025, https://www.indiewire.com/gallery/best-kris-kristofferson-movies/.

41. Phil Hoad, "'I Recently Went Back to the Texas Border—and Urinated on the Wall': How We Made *Lone Star*," *The Guardian*, February 26, 2024, accessed March 15, 2024, https://www.theguardian.com/culture/2024/feb/26/texas-border-wall-lone-star-conflict.

42. Doherty, "Movie Guide Interview."

43. Cast Deal Memo, Matthew McConaughey, May 22, 1995, Screen Arts Mavericks & Makers Collection, University of Michigan Library, Special Collections Research Center, John Sayles Papers, 1959–2013, box 94.

44. Edward Segarra, "Matthew McConaughey Rebelled Against 'Rom-Com Dude' Image by Moving to Texas," *USA Today*, November 20, 2024, accessed January 19, 2025, https://www.usatoday.com/story/entertainment/movies/2024/11/20/matthew-mcconaughey-rom-com-leave-hollywood-texas/76461578007/.

45. "Matthew McConaughey," University of Texas at Austin, Radio-Television-Film, Moody College of Communication, accessed January 19, 2024, https://rtf.utexas.edu/faculty/matthew-mcconaughey.

46. Hoad, "I Recently Went Back."

47. Myron Meisel, "*Lone Star*," Film Journal, June 1996, Sayles Papers, box 94.

48. Sultze, "Rewriting the West," 20.

49. Schimkowitz, "John Sayles on *Lone Star*."

50. Interview, Sayles by Nava.

51. Drew Taylor, "'Lone Star' Director John Sayles on Where the Movie Has Been the Last 30 Years: 'They Go Into Somebody's Closet,'" *The Wrap*, January 18, 2024, accessed July 20, 2024, https://www.thewrap.com/lone-star-john-sayles-criterion-collection-interview/.

52. Stuart Dryburgh Interview (Interviewer is not identified), *Lone Star* Criterion Collection, 2024.

53. "*Lone Star* Continues to Make National News," *Eagle Pass Sunday News*, June 30, 1996.

54. Ratner, "Megan Ratner Discusses."

55. Interview, Sayles by Nava.

56. Meisel, "*Lone Star*."

57. Barr, "The Borders of Time," 369.

58. Interview, Sayles by Nava.

59. Clark-Jones, "*Lone Star*," 60.

60. Washington, "Disturbing the Peace," 15.

61. Ratner, "Megan Ratner Discusses."

62. Sultze, "Rewriting the West," 20.

63. Ratner, "Megan Ratner Discusses."

64. Ratner, "Megan Ratner Discusses."

65. Continuity Polaroids, Sayles Papers, box 96.

66. Caroline Hall Otis, Cast member diary, 8, Sayles Papers, 1959–2013, box 91.

67. Otis, Cast member diary, 23.

68. Otis, Cast member diary, 8.

69. Otis, Cast member diary, 10.

70. Hoad, "I Recently Went Back."

71. "Writing and Directing *Lone Star*: A Talk with John Sayles," *Scenario* 2, no. 2 (1996).

72. "Sam Deeds," Sayles Papers, box 94; Hoad, "I Recently Went Back."

73. Otis, Cast member diary, 10.

74. Otis, Cast member diary, 9.

75. Linehan, "Finding the New Frontier."

76. Ratner, "Megan Ratner Discusses."

77. Letter to Martin Shafer and Liz Glotzer at Castle Rock, September 11, 1995, Sayles Papers, box 96.

78. Otis, Cast member diary, 10.

79. The National Research Group, Inc., Memo from Randy Baker to Martin Shafer, Castle Rock Entertainment, Sayles Papers, box 98.

80. Castle Rock Entertainment, Interoffice Memo, May 17, 1996, Sayles Papers, box 98.

81. Ratner, "Megan Ratner Discusses."

82. Ciaran Carty, "Cork Misses Out on Collins," Sayles Papers.

83. Kenneth Turan, "Master of the Possible: Director John Sayles Exhibits a Determined Vision," *Los Angeles Times*, May 13, 1996.

84. John Brodie, "Sayles' 'Star' Sails to Sony," *Daily Variety*, January 22, 1996.

85. Brodie, "Sayles' 'Star.'"

86. Kevin Jackson, "Return of a Man Called Sayles," *The Independent*, October 13, 1996.

87. Jay Boyer, "Cast and Dialogue Save Dusty Revisionist Western," *Orlando Sentinel*, September 1996.

88. Jackson, "Return of a Man"; Barbara Shulgasser, "'Lone Star' is Classic Sayles—Full of Commitment, Ethics," *SF Gate*, June 21, 1996, accessed January 19, 2025, https://www.sfgate.com/news/article/lone-star-is-classic-sayles-full-of-3136678.php.

89. Roger Ebert, *Lone Star*, July 3, 1996, accessed August 17, 2024, https://www.rogerebert.com/reviews/lone-star-1996.

90. See Jack Ryan, *John Sayles, Filmmaker: A Critical Study of the Independent Writer-Director* (McFarland, 1998); Diane Carson and Heidi Kenaga, *Sayles Talk: New Perspectives on Independent Filmmaker John Sayles* (Wayne State University Press, 2005); Mark Bould, *The Cinema of John Sayles: Lone Star* (Wallflower, 2009); Smith, *Sayles on Sayles*; Diane Carson, ed., *John Sayles: Interviews* (University of Mississippi Press, 1999); Gerald Molyneaux, *John Sayles: An Unauthorized Biography of the Pioneering Indie Filmmaker* (Renaissance Books, 2000).

91. Matthew Carter, "'I'm Just a Cowboy': Transnational Identities of the Borderlands in Tommy Lee Jones' *The Three Burials of Melquiades Estrada*," *European Journal of American Studies* 7, no. 1 (2012): 5.

CHAPTER ONE

1. West and West, "Borders and Boundaries," 14.

2. A. Gabriel Meléndez. M. Jane Young, Patricia Moore, Patrick Pynes, eds. *The Multi-cultural Southwest: A Reader* (University of Arizona Press, 2001), 137.

3. Meléndez et. al., *Multi-cultural Southwest*, 137.

4. Mary Louise Pratt, "Arts of the Contact Zone," in *Profession* (1991): 34.

5. Priscilla Solis Ybarra, *Writing the Good Life: Mexican American Literature and the Environment* (University of Arizona Press, 2016), 37.

6. Rachel Adams, *Continental Divides: Remapping the Cultures of North America* (University of Chicago Press, 2009), 35.

7. Anzaldúa, *Borderlands/La Frontera*, 61.

8. Chamizal National Memorial, Texas, National Park Service: US Department of the Interior, June 8, 2024, accessed August 11, 2024, https://www.nps.gov/cham/learn/historyculture/index.htm.

9. Vantage Point: International Bridge, National Park Service: US Department of the Interior, February 5, 2024, accessed June 9, 2024, https://www.nps.gov/places/vantage-bridge.htm#:~:text=Can%20you%20spot%20the%20%E2%80%9CWelcome,to%20cross%20from%20either%20side.

10. Vantage Point: International Bridge.

11. Patricia Nelson Limerick, *Something in the Soil: Legacies and Reckonings in the New West* (W. W. Norton, 2000), 5.

12. Tobias, "Interview: John Sayles."

13. Anzaldúa, *Borderlands/La Frontera*, 59.

14. Anzaldúa also crosses linguistic borders, moving from English to Castilian Spanish, to regional dialects, to Nahuatl, speaking "the language of the borderlands."

15. Anzaldúa, *Borderlands/La Frontera*, 59.

16. Patricia Nelson Limerick, "The Adventures of the Frontier in the Twentieth Century," in *The Frontier in American Culture*, ed. James R. Grossman (University of California Press, 1994), 75.

17. Richard Aquila, *Wanted Dead or Alive: The American West in Popular Culture* (University of Chicago Press, 1996), 12.

18. Peter Cowie, *John Ford and the American West* (Harry N. Abrams, 2004), 7.

19. Aquila, *Wanted Dead or Alive*, 10.

20. Limerick, *Something in the Soil*, 79.

21. Limerick, *Something in the Soil*, 88–89.

22. Limerick, *Something in the Soil*, 90.

23. Limerick, *Something in the Soil*, 90.

24. Sultze, "Rewriting the West," 20.

25. Campbell, "Forget the Alamo," 166.

26. Barr, "Borders of Time," 368.

27. Dryburgh interview.

28. Bould, *Cinema of John Sayles*, 134.

29. Tomás Sandoval, Jr., "The Burden of History and John Sayles' *Lone Star*," in *Westerns*, ed. Janet Walker (Routledge, 2001), 71–72.

30. Sandoval, "Burden of History," 72.

31. Sandoval, "Burden of History," 72.

32. Washington, "'Disturbing the Peace,'" 16.

33. Smith, *Sayles on Sayles*, 218.

34. Sandoval, "Burden of History," 72.

35. Sandoval, "Burden of History," 72.
36. Sandoval, "Burden of History," 72.
37. Washington, "'Disturbing the Peace," 14.
38. Doherty, "Movie Guide Interview."
39. "Eladio Cruz," Sayles Papers, box 94.
40. Sultze, "Rewriting the West," 24.
41. "Young Chuco Montoya," Sayles Papers, box 94.
42. "Eladio Cruz," Sayles Papers, box 94.
43. Sayles Papers, box 94.
44. A Tejano refers to a person living in Texas who is of Mexican descent and has lived in the region before it became an independent republic.
45. José E. Limón, "Tex-Sex-Mex: American Identities, Lone Stars and the Politics of Racialized Sexuality," in *American Identities*, National Imaginaries, eds. Larry J. Reynolds and Gordon Hutner (Princeton University Press, 2001), 229.
46. See John M. Nieto-Phillips, *The Language of Blood: The Making of Spanish-American Identity in New Mexico, 1880s–1930s* (University of New Mexico Press, 2004); and Charles Montgomery, *The Spanish Redemption: Heritage, Power, and Loss on New Mexico's Upper Rio Grande* (University of California Press, 2002), 229.
47. Spanish-American identity is distinct from other identities such as "Mexican American," "Chicano," "Latino," and "Hispanic," as each signals distinctive connections to heritage in Latin America and Spain and carry political and social implications. For instance, Frank G. Pérez and Carlos F. Ortega explain that "Mexican American" identity indicates Americans of Mexican descent, whereas those that identify as "Chicana/o" see themselves as members of "historically and structurally oppressed group and advocate for social justice." Both "Hispanic" and "Spanish-American" identities, though carrying different class connotations, downplay Indigenous ancestry and generally "share a cultural orientation that supports the fantasy heritage of the Southwest."
48. See Carey McWilliams, *North to Mexico: The Spanish-Speaking People of the United States*, 3rd ed. (Praeger, 2016), chap. 2.

49. Sayles Papers, box 94.

50. Dryburgh interview.

51. "Mercedes Cruz," Sayles Papers, box 94.

52. Lisa Lowe, *Immigrant Acts: On Asian American Cultural Politics* (Duke University Press, 1999), 2.

53. Sandoval, "Burden of History," 72.

54. Washington, "Disturbing the Peace."

55. Interview, Sayles by Nava.

56. Tobias, "Interview: John Sayles on 'Lone Star.'

57. Otis, Cast member diary, 15.

58. Marine Soubeille, "Transnational Identity on the contemporary Texas-Mexico Border in Tejano (David Blue Garcia, 2018)," In *Transnationalism and Imperialism: Endurance of the Global Western Film*, eds. Hervé Mayer and David Roche (Indiana University Press, 2022), 84.

59. Slotkin, *Gunfighter Nation*, 486.

60. Tobias, "Interview."

61. Tobias, "Interview.'

62. Carter, "'I'm Just a Cowboy,'" 5.

63. Carter, "'I'm Just a Cowboy,'" 5.

64. Daniel M. Gold, "'Western' Chronicles Borderland Traditions, Both Charming and Violent," *New York Times*, September 24, 2015, accessed August 26, 2024, https://www.nytimes.com/2015/09/25/movies/review-western-chronicles-borderland-traditions-both-charming-and-violent.html?partner=rss&emc=rss.

65. Campbell, *Post-Westerns*, 329–30.

66. Campbell, *Post-Westerns*, 331.

67. Soubeille, "Transnational Identity," 85.

68. Schimkowitz, "John Sayles on *Lone Star*."

69. Tobias, "Interview."

70. Tobias, "Interview."

71. Interview, Sayles by Nava.

CHAPTER TWO

1. Marita Sturken, *Tangled Memories: The Vietnam War, the Aids Epidemic, and the Politics of Remembering* (University of California Press, 1997), 3.

2. Sultze, "Rewriting the West," 20.

3. Sultze, "Rewriting the West," 21.

4. Campbell. "'Forget the Alamo,'" 167.

5. Otis, Cast member diary, 32.

6. Campbell, "'Forget the Alamo,'" 162.

7. Interview, Sayles by Nava.

8. Sulze, "Rewriting the West," 21.

9. Washington, "'Disturbing the Peace,'" 13.

10. Sultze, "Rewriting the West," 22.

11. Smith, *Sayles on Sayles*, 218.

12. Smith, *Sayles on Sayles*, 229

13. Richard Barsam and Dave Monahan, *Looking at Movies: An Introduction to Film*, 3rd ed. (W. W. Norton, 2009), 7.

14. Sultze, "Rewriting the West," 23.

15. Janet Walker, "Captive Images in the Traumatic Western: *The Searchers, Pursued, Once Upon A Time in the West*, and *Lone Star*," in *Westerns*, ed. Walker, 246.

16. Hoad, "'I Recently Went Back."

17. Sultze, "Rewriting the West," 22.

18. Ratner, "Megan Ratner Discusses."

19. Walker, "Captive Images," 246.

20. Walker, "Captive Images," 221.

21. Schimkowitz, "John Sayles on *Lone Star*."

22. Otis, Cast member diary, 24.

23. Sulze, "Rewriting the West," 21.

24. Susan Felleman, "Oedipus Edits (*Lone Star*)," in *Sayles Talk*, 170.

25. Barr, "The Borders of Time," 369.

26. Tarancón de Francisco, "Film Genre," 412–13.

27. Sulze, "Rewriting the West," 21.

28. Dryburgh interview.

29. Otis, Cast member diary, 15.

30. Kitses, *Horizons West*, 29.

31. "Fenton," Sayles Papers, box 94.

32. "Danny," Sayles Papers, box 94.

33. Erika Doss, *Memorial Mania: Public Feeling In America* (University of Chicago Press, 2010), 2.

34. "Young Sam," Sayles Papers, box 94.

35. "Young Sam," Sayles Papers, box 94.

36. Black Mama, White Mama features a black prisoner, and a white prisoner handcuffed together while they escape from jail, a choice Sayles made to underscore how different races are linked together, regardless of their desire.

37. Scripts, draft 4/5/1995, Sayles Papers, box 94.

38. "Monumental Lies," *Reveal News*, 15 August 2020, accessed March 20, 2021, https://revealnews.org/podcast/monumental-lies-update-2/.

39. Marita Sturken, *Terrorism in American Memory: Memorials, Museums, and Architecture in the Post 9/11 Era* (NYU Press, 2022), 1.

40. See Alison Fields, "Visualizing Juan de Oñate's Colonial Legacies in New Mexico," *Journal of Genocide Research* 24, no. 4 (2022): 471–87.

41. Campbell, "'Forget the Alamo,'" 163.

42. Mihaly Csikszentmihalyi, "Why We Need Things," in *History from Things*, eds. Steven Lubar and W. David Kingery (Smithsonian Institution Press, 1987), 22.

43. Otis, Cast member diary, 30.

44. "Young Otis," Sayles Papers, box 94.

45. "Delmore," Sayles Papers, box 94.

46. "Delmore," Sayles Papers, box 94.

47. Anna Adams, "Forget the Alamo: Thinking about History in John Sayles' *Lone Star*," *History Teacher* 40, no. 3 (2007): 343.

48. Sulze, "Rewriting the West," 22.

49. Barr, "Borders of Time," 373.

50. Otis, Cast member diary, 20.

51. John Sayles and Gavin Smith, eds., *Sayles on Sayles* (Faber and Faber, 1998), 218.

52. Sayles and Smith, *Sayles on Sayles,* 218.

53. Walker, "Captive Images," 247.

54. Limón, "Tex-Sex-Mex," 242.

55. Limón, "Tex-Sex-Mex," 242.

56. Interview, Sayles by Nava.

57. Bould, *Cinema of John Sayles,* 134.

58. Kim Magowan, "'Blood Only Means What You Let It': Incest and Miscegenation in John Sayles's *Lone Star,*" *Film Quarterly* 57, no. 1 (2003): 20.

59. Todd F. Davis and Kenneth Womack, "Forget the Alamo: Reading the Ethics of Style in John Sayles's *Lone Star,*" *Style in Cinema* 32 no. 3 (1998): 471.

60. Sayles and Smith, *Sayles on Sayles,* 227–28.

61. Sayles and Smith, *Sayles on Sayles,* 218.

62. Magowan, "'Blood Only Means,'" 23.

63. Magowan, "'Blood Only Means,'" 27.

64. Ruth Barton, "*Lone Star,*" *Film Ireland,* October/November 1996, 38.

65. Campbell, "'Forget the Alamo,'" 175–76.

66. Magowan, "'Blood Only Means,'" 23.

CHAPTER THREE

1. Washington, "'Disturbing the Peace,'" 12–13.

2. Steven Dubin, *Displays of Power: Controversy in the American Museum from the Enola Gay to Sensation* (NYU Press, 1999), 153–54.

3. Dubin, *Displays of Power,* 156.

4. Dubin, *Displays of Power,* 157.

5. "Minnie Bledsoe," Sayles Papers, box 94.

6. "Wesley Birdsong," Sayles Papers, box 94.

7. Washington, "'Disturbing the Peace,'" 13.

8. Sultze, "Rewriting the West," 21.

9. Sultze, "Rewriting the West," 21.

10. "Cody," Sayles Papers, box 94.

11. Magowan, "'Blood Only Means,'" 24.
12. Magowan, "'Blood Only Means,'" 24–25.
13. Clark-Jones, "*Lone Star*," 59.
14. "Jorge," Sayles Papers, box 94.
15. "Jorge," Sayles Papers, box 94.
16. "Sam Deeds," Sayles Papers, box 94.
17. "Charley Wade," Sayles Papers, box 94.
18. Magowan, "'Blood Only Means,'" 22.
19. "Charley Wade," Sayles Papers, box 94.
20. "Minnie Bledsoe," Sayles Papers, box 94.
21. Clark-Jones, "*Lone Star*," 59.
22. Clark-Jones, "*Lone Star*," 59.
23. Barr, "Borders of Time," 369.
24. Washington, "'Disturbing the Peace,'" 14.
25. "Ray," Sayles Papers, box 94.
26. Schimkowitz, "John Sayles on *Lone Star*," AV Club, January 16, 2024.
27. "Forget the Alamo: John Sayles' *Lone Star* Will Force You to Look at Texas History in a Way You Never Thought You Would," *FW Weekly*, June 20–27, 1996.
28. Interview, Sayles by Nava.
29. "Forget the Alamo."
30. Clark-Jones, "*Lone Star*," 58.
31. Clark-Jones, "*Lone Star*," 59.
32. Washington, "'Disturbing the Peace,'" 16.
33. Washington, "'Disturbing the Peace,'" 16.
34. Bould, *Cinema of John Sayles*, 140.
35. Washington, "'Disturbing the Peace,'" 16.
36. Barr, "Borders of Time," 369.
37. Bould, *Cinema of John Sayles*, 138.
38. Washington, "'Disturbing the Peace,'" 16.
39. Clark-Jones, "*Lone Star*," 61.
40. Campbell, "'Forget the Alamo,'" 163.
41. Campbell, "'Forget the Alamo,'" 163.

42. Campbell, "'Forget the Alamo,'" 163.

43. Bould, *Cinema of John Sayles*, 136.

44. Sneha Day, "1836 Project Promotes Sanitized Version of Texas History," *Texas Tribune*, September 26, 2022, accessed August 24, 2024, https://www.texastribune.org/2022/09/26/texas-1836-project-pamphlet/.

45. Richard Slotkin, "John Ford's Stagecoach and the Mythic Space of the Western Movie," in *The Big Empty*, ed. Leonard Engel (University of New Mexico Press, 1994), 276.

46. Kitses, *Horizons West*, 31.

47. John Bodnar, *Remaking America: Public Memory, Commemoration, and Patriotism in the Twentieth Century* (Princeton University Press, 1992), 13.

48. Campbell, "Forget the Alamo," 165.

49. Davis and Womack, "Forget the Alamo," 473–74.

50. Smith, *Sayles on Sayles*, 224.

51. Sandoval, "Burden of History," 72.

52. Davis and Womack, "Forget the Alamo," 474.

53. Smith, *Sayles on Sayles*, 223.

54. Smith, *Sayles on Sayles*, 223.

55. Adams, *Continental Divides*, 91.

56. "Athena," Sayles Papers, box 94.

57. "Delmore," Sayles Papers, box 94.

58. "Delmore," Sayles Papers, box 94.

59. Neil Campbell. "'Forget the Alamo,'" 164.

60. Campbell, "'Forget the Alamo,'" 171.

61. Interview, Sayles by Nava.

62. Campbell, "'Forget the Alamo,'" 176.

63. Washington, "'Disturbing the Peace,'" 13.

64. Amy Lonetree, *Decolonizing Museums: Representing Native America in National and Tribal Museums*, Lincoln: (University of Nebraska Press, 2012), 5–6.

CHAPTER FOUR

1. Quoted in Limerick, *Something in the Soil*, 82. Full text available at Yale Law School, The Avalon Project: Documents in Law, History, and Diplomacy, accessed August 24, 2024, https://avalon.law.yale.edu/20th_century/reagan2.asp.

2. Limerick, *Something in the Soil*, 81.

3. Julie Musbach, "Guadalupe Cultural Arts Center Presents 'The Other Side of the Alamo: Art Against the Myth,'" *Broadway World*, February 22, 2018, accessed August 25, 2024, https://www.broadwayworld.com/article/Guadalupe-Cultural-Arts-Center-Presents-The-Other-Side-of-the-Alamo-Art-Against-the-Myth-20180222.

4. Morgan O'Hanlon, "In San Antonio, 'The Other Side of the Alamo' Turns Whitewashed Texas History on its Head," *Texas Observer*, April 2, 2018, accessed August 25, 2024, https://www.texasobserver.org/in-san-antonio-the-other-side-of-the-alamo-turns-whitewashed-texas-history-on-its-head/.

5. Stephen Oleszek, "Chicanx Artists Challenge the Mythology of the Alamo," Hyperallergic, September 20, 2018, accessed August 25, 2024, https://hyperallergic.com/460874/chicanx-artists-challenge-the-mythology-of-the-alamo/.

6. Oleszek, "Chicanx Artists Challenge the Mythology of the Alamo."

7. Ruben C. Cordova, "José Esquivel, Pioneering Chicano Artist, Part 2: The Return to Chicano Art, 1991–2022," *Glasstire*, April 16, 2023, accessed August 25, 2024, https://glasstire.com/2023/04/16/jose-esquivel-pioneering-chicano-artist-part-2-the-return-to-chicano-art-1991-2022/.

8. Luis Valderas, "Black Dream Space," accessed August 26, 2024. https://www.luisvalderasartist.com/black-dream-place.

9. Postcommodity, Repellent Fence, 2015, accessed August 26, 2024, https://postcommodity.com/Repellent_Fence_English.html.

10. Postcommodity, Repellent Fence, 2015.

11. "About," La Frontera: Artists Across the US/Mexico Border, https://borderartists.com/about/.

12. Bill Chappell, "Seesaws Built on U.S. Border Wall Win Prestigious Design Prize," NPR, January 19, 2021, accessed September 1, 2024, https://www.npr.org/2021/01/19/958339302/see-saws-built-on-u-s-border-wall-win-prestigious-design-prize.

FILMOGRAPHY

The Ballad of Gregorio Cortez (Robert M. Young, 1982)
The Bridge (TV series, Meredith Stiehm and Elwood Reid, 2013–2014)
El Norte (Gregory Nava, 1983)
A Fistful of Dollars (Sergio Leone, 1964)
High Noon (Fred Zinneman, 1952)
The Magnificent Seven (John Sturges, 1960)
The Man Who Shot Liberty Valance (John Ford, 1962)
My Darling Clementine (John Ford, 1946)
No Country for Old Men (Joel and Ethan Coen, 2007)
The Outlaw Josey Wales (Clint Eastwood, 1976)
The Searchers (John Ford, 1956)
Sicario (Denis Villeneuve, 2015)
Shane (George Stevens, 1953)
Stagecoach (John Ford, 1939)
Tejano (David Blue Garcia, 2018)
The Three Burials of Melquiades Estrada (Tommy Lee Jones, 2005)
Touch of Evil (Orson Welles, 1968)
Unforgiven (Clint Eastwood, 1992)
Western (Bill and Turner Ross, 2015)
The Wild Bunch (Sam Peckinpah, 1969)

SELECTED BIBLIOGRAPHY

BOOKS AND ARTICLES

Adams, Anna. "Forget the Alamo: Thinking about History in John Sayles' *Lone Star*." *History Teacher*, 40, no. 3 (2007): 339–47.

Adams, Rachel. *Continental Divides: Remapping the Cultures of North America.* University of Chicago Press, 2009.

Anzaldúa, Gloria. *Borderlands/La Frontera: The New Mestiza. The Critical Edition,* edited by Ricardo F. Vivancos-Pérez and Norma Cantú, Aunt Lute Books, 2021.

Aquila, Richard. *Wanted Dead or Alive: The American West in Popular Culture.* University of Chicago Press, 1996.

Barr, Alan P. "The Borders of Time, Place, and People in John Sayles's *Lone Star*." *Journal of American Studies*, 37, no. 3 (2003): 365–74.

Barsam, Richard, and Dave Monahan. *Looking at Movies: An Introduction to Film*. 3rd ed. W. W. Norton, 2009.

Bartley, William. "'Not by a Long Shot': John Sayles's *Lone Star*, the Future, and the Bildungsroman." *Canadian Review of American Studies* 50, no. 1 (2020): 165–91.

Bodnar, John. *Remaking America: Public Memory, Commemoration, and Patriotism in the Twentieth Century*. Princeton University Press, 1992.

Bould, Mark. *The Cinema of John Sayles: Lone Star*. Wallflower, 2009.

Campbell, Neil. "'Forget the Alamo': History, Legend, and Memory in John Sayles' *Lone Star*." In *Memory and Popular Film*, edited by Paul Grainge. Manchester University Press, 2003.

———. *Post-Westerns: Cinema, Region, West*. University of Nebraska Press, 2013.

Carson, Diane, ed. *John Sayles: Interviews*. University of Mississippi Press, 1999.

———, and Heidi Kenaga. *Sayles Talk: New Perspectives on Independent Filmmaker John Sayles*. Wayne State University Press, 2005.

Carter, Matthew. "I'm Just a Cowboy": Transnational Identities of the Borderlands in Tommy Lee Jones' *The Three Burials of Melquiades Estrada*." *European Journal of American Studies* 7, no. 1 (2012): 2–15.

Clark-Jones, Melissa. "*Lone Star*: Renovation of the American Dream." *Studies in Popular Culture* 20, no. 3 (1998): 57–69.

Cowie, Peter. *John Ford and the American West*. Harry N. Abrams, 2004.

Csikszentmihalyi, Mihaly. "Why We Need Things." In *History from Things: Essays on Material Culture*, edited by Steven Lubar and W. David Kingery. Smithsonian Institution Press, 1987.

Davis, Todd F., and Kenneth Womack. "Forget the Alamo: Reading the Ethics of Style in John Sayles's *Lone Star*." *Style in Cinema* 32, no. 3 (1998): 471–85.

Doss, Erika. *Memorial Mania: Public Feeling In America*. University of Chicago Press, 2010.

Dubin, Steven. *Displays of Power: Controversy in the American Museum from the Enola Gay to Sensation*. NYU Press, 1999.

Engel, Leonard, ed. *The Big Empty: Essays on the Land as Narrative*. University of New Mexico Press, 1994.

Fields, Alison. "Visualizing Juan de Oñate's Colonial Legacies in New Mexico." *Journal of Genocide Research* 24, no. 4 (2022): 471–87.

Flores, Richard R. *Remembering the Alamo: Memory, Modernity, and the Master Symbol*. University of Texas Press, 2002.

Kitses, Jim. *Horizons West: Directing the Western from John Ford to Clint Eastwood*. British Film Institute, 2004.

———, and Gregg Rickman, eds. *The Western Reader*. Limelight, 1998.

Limerick, Paticia Nelson. *Something in the Soil: Legacies and Reckonings in the New West*. W. W. Norton, 2000.

———. "The Adventures of the Frontier in the Twentieth Century." In *The Frontier in American Culture*, edited by James R. Grossman, 67–102. University of California Press, 1994.

Limón, José E. "Tex-Sex-Mex: American Identities, Lone Stars and the Politics of Racialized Sexuality." In *National Imaginaries, American Identities: The Cultural Work of American Iconography*, edited by Larry J. Reynolds and Gordon Hutner. Princeton University Press, 2001.

Lonetree, Amy. *Decolonizing Museums: Representing Native America in National and Tribal Museums*. University of Nebraska Press, 2012.

Lowe, Lisa. *Immigrant Acts: On Asian American Cultural Politics*. Duke University Press, 1999.

Magowan, Kim. "'Blood Only Means What You Let It': Incest and Miscegenation in John Sayles's *Lone Star*." *Film Quarterly* 57, no. 1 (2003): 20–31.

McGee, Patrick. *From Shane to Kill Bill: Rethinking the Western*. Blackwell, 2007.

McWilliams, Carey. *North to Mexico: The Spanish-Speaking People of the United States*. 3rd ed. Praeger, 2016.

Meléndez, A. Gabriel et al., eds. *The Multi-cultural Southwest: A Reader*. University of Arizona Press, 2001.

Mitchell, Lee Clark. *Late Westerns: The Persistence of a Genre*. University of Nebraska Press, 2018.

Molyneaux, Gerald. *John Sayles: An Unauthorized Biography of the Pioneering Indie Filmmaker*. Renaissance Books, 2000.

Pratt, Mary Louise. "Arts of the Contact Zone." *Profession*. MLA, 1991.

Radway, Janice. "What's in a Name? Presidential Address to the American Studies Association, 20 November 1998." *American Quarterly* 51, no. 1 (1999): 1–32.

Rollins, Peter C., and John E. O'Connor, eds. *Hollywood's West: The American Frontier in Film, Television, and History*. University Press of Kentucky, 2005.

Ryan, Jack. *John Sayles, Filmmaker: A Critical Study of the Independent Writer-Director*. McFarland, 1998.

Sandoval, Jr., Tomás. "The Burden of History and John Sayle's *Lone Star*." In *Westerns: Films Through History*, edited by Janet Walker, 71–85. Routledge, 2001.

Sayles, John. *Thinking in Pictures: The Making of the Movie Matewan*. De Capo Press, 1987.

Schatz, Thomas. *Hollywood Genres: Formulas, Filmmaking, and the Studio System*. Random House, 1981.

Slotkin, Richard. *Gunfighter Nation: The Myth of the Frontier in Twentieth-Century America*. University of Oklahoma Press, 1998.

Smith, Gavin, ed. *Sayles on Sayles*. Faber and Faber, 1998.

Solis Ybarra, Priscilla. *Writing the Goodlife: Mexican American Literature and the Environment*. University of Arizona Press, 2016.

Soubeille, Marine. "Transnational Identity on the Contemporary Texas-Mexico Border in *Tejano* (David Blue Garcia, 2018)." In *Transnationalism and Imperialism: Endurance of the Global Western Film*, edited by Hervé Mayer and David Roche. Indiana University Press, 2022.

Sturken, Marita. *Tangled Memories: The Vietnam War, the Aids Epidemic, and the Politics of Remembering*. University of California Press, 1997.

———. *Terrorism in American Memory: Memorials, Museums, and Architecture in the Post 9/11 Era*. NYU Press, 2022.

Sultze, Kimberly. "Rewriting the West as Multi-Cultural: Legend Meets Complex Histories in la Frontera in John Sayles' *Lone Star*." *Film & History* 33, no. 2 (2003): 19–25.

Tarancón De Francisco, Juan A. "Film Genre and the Power of Symbolic Thought: The Challenge to the Natural History Paradigm in John Sayles' *Lone Star*." *Quarterly Review of Film and Video* 29, no. 5 (2012): 409–18.

Washington, Mary Helen. "'Disturbing the Peace: What Happens to American Studies If You Put African American Studies at the Center?': Presidential Address to the American Studies Association, October 29, 1997." *American Quarterly* 50 no. 1 (1998): 1–23.

West, Dennis et al. "Borders and Boundaries: An Interview with John Sayles." *Cinéaste* 22, no. 3 (1996): 14–17.

SPECIAL COLLECTIONS

Screen Arts Mavericks and Makers Collection, The University of Michigan, John Sayles Papers.